head first

Some of the amazing things people have to say about Tony Buzan:

"Tony Buzan will do for the brain what Stephen Hawking did for the universe."
The Times

"The whole world should Mind Map®."
The Express

"If you put Buzan's theories to the test, you could find yourself memorizing pages from a phone book or becoming the brainiest person in the world."
PC World Magazine

"Buzan's mental technology is five years ahead of the game. Any company using it will inevitably gain a competitive edge."
IBM, New York

"More than a few serious minds out there are paying attention."
International Herald Tribune

HEAD FIRST

10 Ways to Tap into Your Natural Genius

TONY BUZAN

Thorsons

Thorsons
An Imprint of HarperCollins*Publishers*
77–85 Fulham Palace Road,
Hammersmith, London W6 8JB

The Thorsons website address is:
www.thorsons.com

and *Thorsons*
are trademarks of
HarperCollins*Publishers* Limited

First published 2000
This edition 2002

10 9 8 7 6 5 4 3 2 1

© Tony Buzan 2000

Tony Buzan asserts the moral right to be
identified as author of this work

Mind Maps® is a registered trademark of the Buzan Organization

Plate section illustrations by Alan and Emily Burton

ISBN 0 00 713285 9

Printed and bound in Great Britain by
Bath Press Colourbooks, Glasgow

This book is dedicated to all those who are developing their Multiple Intelligences. By doing so you are helping to create a new global Renaissance, and are transforming the 21st century into the Century of the Brain, and the third millennium into the Millennium of the Mind.

contents

ACKNOWLEDGEMENTS

I wish to thank my two teams, who by the application of their own Multiple Intelligences helped *Head First* to become a best seller before it even hit the book stores. My Thorsons team, including my Commissioning Editor, Carole Tonkinson, who went "Head First" for *Head First* and who worked her heart and soul out to bring it to fruition; my Editor, Charlotte Ridings, who grasped the concept immediately, and who honed it so well; to Paul Redhead, Toby Watson, Tim Byrne, Yvette Cowles, Jo Lal, Megan Slyfield, Jacqui Caulton and Aislinn McCormick, you are a fabulous team to work with. Dedicated, intelligent and very creative. My thanks.

There is also my personal team, including especially my Publications Manager, Caroline Shott, without whose dedication and creative input *Head First* would not exist; to my External Editor, Vanda North, *Head First*'s ideal compassionate midwife through pregnancy and birth; to my Personal Assistant and dear friend, Lesley Bias, who worked far beyond the call of duty to help everybody meet their deadlines; to the Art and Mind Map® Magicians, Alan and Emily Burton, who make visual dreams come true; and to my dear Mum, Jean Buzan, the best proof-reader I have ever met!

LIST OF MIND MAPS®

FOREWORD

The amazing story of Scott Hagwood

An amazing thing happened at the 2001 American Memory Championships.

The local organisers had told me that Tatiana Cooley, the reigning United States Memory Champion, had some serious challengers.

Among them were a senior executive from Con Edison, three university students who had been training for the event in the same way as you might for the New York Marathon, a senior engineer from General Electric, and a number of outsiders who reckoned their chances were good.

The championship consists of five major events, including the memorisation of: a gigantic shopping list; 100 names and faces in fifteen minutes; a previously unpublished poem; a 1000-digit number; and a pack of cards, to be memorised in less than five minutes – an accomplishment that no American, including Tatiana, had ever achieved in open competition.

After the first event, the engineer from General Electric had shot into the lead, with the challenging pack close behind.

In the second and third events the engineer did well, although his lead was diminishing, and Tatiana was becoming his main challenger.

In the fourth event, Tatiana crushed her opposition, and went into a commanding lead. The challengers for the silver and bronze positions were all clustered together, with seven competitors capable of taking the silver and bronze.

Only the speed memorisation of the deck of cards was remaining. It was then that the audience and myself were told the amazing story of the engineer from General Electric, who at that stage was in second place, but only just.

The story was astonishing, and was a wonderful example of the application of multiple intelligences to the major challenges of life.

Two years before the championships, the engineer, Scott Hagwood, 36 years old and living in Fayetteville, Tenessee, was told that he had serious cancer of the thyroid.

He was told also that the cancer would require heavy radiocative and chemotherapy treatment. The treatments, his doctors said, would massively sap his physical energy, and reduce the effectiveness of all his mental skills and activity, especially memory.

Rather than "give in" to the horror of his situation, Scott immediately went out and bought a virtual library of books on the brain, learning, Mind Mapping and especially memory.

Rather than letting the treatment obliterate his memory and mental functions, Scott decided to use the power of his brain to stem the tide of forgetting. *"I was worried about losing focus."* said Scott. *"I worried, would I be able to rebound mentally? In isolation, you start to worry about things excessively. I had a lot of family and spiritual support, but I needed to keep my mind sharp."*

Using my techniques, Scott developed his Sensual Intelligence, his Creative Intelligence, his Physical Intelligence, his Personal Intelligence and his Verbal and Mathematical Intelligences.

Scott loved the learning process of improving his mind and his intelligences. He said *"I call it visual music. A musician can take notes on a page and turn them into music. I learnt to take information and turn it into images in my mind."*

The final competition was the five-minute memorisation of a deck of cards. The American record was 28. Tatiana's best was 18. To win, all she needed to do was equal her best and no one other than Scott could possibly beat her. Scott's task however, looked "impossible".

In the final competition, Tatiana immediately came in with an excellent score – she beat her own best by one, memorising 19 cards in sequence perfectly. Only four other people did better than she did, but they were so far behind that it made no difference to the final standings. All the results came in fairly quickly, with the exception of Scott's. He was taking every possible second of the 10 minutes he had in which to recall, and had already got to 24 cards perfectly memorised. But he still had more than half a deck to go in order to beat Tatiana. The lady who was checking his answers was already beginning to perspire profusely, and the entire audience and the many television cameras zoomed in on the two of them as he answered and she checked.

On and on the answering went, Scott getting to 30, then to 35, then to 40. Only Scott's arbiter knew whether he had made any mistakes, and she could only tell him, according to the rules, at the end of his memorisation attempt. The suspense was unbearable, and Scott's time was running out. He got to 48 with only 20 seconds left, and then rattled off the last four.

Had he done it? Had he become the first American ever to have memorised a pack of cards in under five minutes? Was he the new American Memory Champion? Had Tatiana, whose total championship score was already a new American record in itself, been "pipped at the post" by an extraordinary human being?

Yes! Yes! Yes! and Yes! Scott's arbiter leapt out of her chair screaming *"He's done it! He's done it! Perfect! Perfect! Perfect!"*

By using and developing his amazing multiple intelligences under the most trying of conditions, Scott Hagwood had become a giant figure in the annals of Mind and Memory Sports.

"It's like a dream, and I keep expecting to wake up." said Scott.

He also said, and this, dear reader, is most important for you to know, that what he could do anyone could do, as long as they had the correct formulas for using their brains and their multiple intelligences.

In *Head First* you have the first operations manual for your multiple intelligences. Enjoy the journey!

a letter to my readers

When I was a young boy at school, I found myself perplexed and confused by many questions to which I found I had no answers, and demotivated by comments from my teachers that seemed to confirm my lack of intelligence, concentration and energy.

My unanswered questions included the following:

- Why were things like geography, history, English, and science considered more important than sports, art, and music?
- Why was it that some boys (whom we all considered brilliant) were thought by our teachers to be disruptive and stupid, while some boys whom we thought to have no common sense at all, were considered bright by our teachers?
- Why would I sometimes get a lower mark in a test in which I knew I knew more than other students who, for some inexplicable reason got higher marks than me?
- Conversely, why would I sometimes get a higher mark in a test than someone whom I knew knew more than I did?

My teachers' comments about my general academic career included:

- "Lazy."
- "Tends to day-dream too much."
- "Poor powers of concentration."
- "This young boy is obviously not talented in art."
- "Can be a disruptive influence in class."
- "Failed to live up to expectations – a disappointing performance."
- "Shows no aptitude for PE [Physical Education]."
- "Performance in history appalling – shows little interest or talent in this subject."
- "Non-college material!"
- "Could do better."

Sound familiar?

My unresolved questions gradually clarified themselves over time into three far more focused and incisive points:

1 Who says who is intelligent?
2 Who is the authority that defines what intelligence is?
3 Can IQ be changed for the better?

My attempts to answer these questions became my life's work, and led me to spend the next 30 years exploring the brain and the processes of intelligence, and inventing the concept of Mind Maps® to improve our intelligences.

Head First is really written as a rescue operation for all those brains on Planet Earth who have raised the same questions and/or received similar comments on their report cards!

Enjoy the rediscovery of your natural intelligences!

Tony Buzan

THE CHALLENGE

In the 1950s, Alan Turing, the inventor of the computer, challenged the computer industry to create a machine that was as intelligent as a human being.

The test was, and is, as follows: three knowledgeable and intelligent human beings were to sit facing a curtained barrier. Behind the curtain were another three intelligences: two humans and one computer. All three pairs were to engage in conversation on any topic chosen by the first three people. A prize would be awarded if the computer could convince each of the three people in front of the curtain, in turn, that it was one of the two humans behind the barrier! As this new century begins, no one has even come close to claiming that prize.

Dramatic as it is, and successful as it has been, the Turing Test (as you will discover) has missed at least 90 per cent of the point!

The challenge was based on the old assumption that IQ and human intelligence were primarily based on the power of words. We now know that this is only one of many intelligences that we have, and that for a computer to prove that it is equal to your human brain, it must demonstrate skills in all 10 intelligences simultaneously – for a computer to combine numerical, physical, sensory, creative and spatial intelligences would be a far more appropriate demonstration of human-like intelligence!

It seems as if the prize will stay unclaimed for a good while yet.

introduction

head first and you

Head First is a revolutionary new book based on the latest research into your brain and body. This research has uncovered the fact that you have far more than the one standard IQ (Intelligence Quotient) everyone has heard about – you actually have 10!

Having a high traditional IQ, based on measures of your verbal and numerical skills, does not automatically equal personal or professional success. Recently there has been a growing acknowledgement of how important *other* skills are in life: the ability to communicate with others, to persevere, to plan and balance one's life, and so on. In *Head First* I will guide you on an exploration of these other intelligences. I will show you how you can develop and expand each one of your 10 intelligences: it will transform your abilities!

A BRIEF HISTORY OF INTELLIGENCE

The history of the development of our knowledge about intelligence is fascinating. Although leading thinkers had been searching for a long time for any clues as to "what makes us tick?" and "what makes us smart?," amazingly, the concept of the Intelligence Quotient has been around for less than 100 years – the first experiments in intelligence testing by "scientific means" started only at the beginning of the 20th century.

Some of the early experiments were a little eccentric: measuring knee-jerk response time to see whether the faster your reactions were meant the smarter you were; relating height to intelligence; and measuring bumps on the scalp to see if any of them were "smart" bumps. However, a French psychologist, Alfred Binet, did eventually come up with the first, genuinely scientific method for objectively measuring intelligence. It involved setting standard verbal and numerical tests, with the scores measured against an average of 100. (Binet's test is explained in more detail on page **153**.)

Binet's IQ tests were accepted without question for over 60 years, but by the 1970s, ideas about intelligence were beginning to change. Professor Howard Gardner, Professor Robert Ornstein, myself and others became aware that there are a number of *different* kinds of intelligence, and that each different intelligence acted in harmony with each of the others when they were properly developed.

A truly intelligent person is not one who can simply spout words and numbers; it is someone who can react "intelligently" to all the opportunities, stimulations and problems provided by the environment. Real intelligence means engaging your brain with every aspect of life – you play sport with your brain; you relate to others brain-to-brain; you make love with your brain. All of life is, in fact, lived *Head First*!

YOUR INTELLIGENCES

Your 10 intelligences can be divided into three major categories: your Creative and Emotional Intelligences; your Bodily Intelligences; and your Traditional IQ Intelligences. *Head First* is thus sub-divided into three Parts:

Part 1 – The Creative and Emotional Intelligences

1 **Create Yourself – Creative Intelligence.** Creativity was once thought to be a "magic gift" possessed by only the few. We now know that it *is* a magic gift – possessed by *everyone*. Unleashing the power of your Creative Intelligence is simply a matter of understanding how to do this.

2 **You And You – Personal Intelligence – Your "Satisfaction-With-Yourself" IQ.** It is possible to rank very highly in certain intelligences, but still to be unhappy within yourself. By exploring the nature of Personal Intelligence, *Head First* shows you how your brain can become its own best friend.

3 **You and Them – Social Intelligence – Your "Communication" IQ.** This chapter, dealing with what many experts consider to be the most important of all your intelligences, also confronts one of the world's greatest fears.

4 **Heaven Knows! – Spiritual Intelligence.** Here we explore the meaning of spiritual intelligence, and put into context the growing global trend of spiritual growth.

Part 2 – The Bodily Intelligences

5 **Body Talk – Physical Intelligence.** In light of new research on the brain/body connection, the "all brawn no brain" syndrome is being transformed into "a healthy body equals a healthy mind." In *Head First* your body ties for first!

6 **Making Sense of Your Senses – Sensual Intelligence.** It was once thought that your five senses were static and unchanging receptors of information from the world around you. State-of-the-art science now shows us that each

THE ULTIMATE *HEAD FIRST* INTELLIGENCE STAR – LEONARDO DA VINCI

Leonardo da Vinci is regularly given as the best example of the "all round genius"; in other words, as the individual who has most dramatically demonstrated the use of all his intelligences. Leonardo's genius was so great that some people rate him the greatest genius of all time in many of the individual intelligences too. He was almost entirely self-taught, and provides a tremendous example to us of just what someone can achieve with a determination to expand and develop all of his intelligences.

Contrary to many assumptions, Leonardo was not from a wealthy, well-to-do family, and his formal education was very basic. When he was a boy, he was apprenticed to a painter/sculptor, in whose workshop he learned his craft of drawing and painting.

Leonardo himself said that he became the "genius" that he was because of the application of his brain to learning how it – and especially his senses – worked. As you read *Head First*, constantly bear Leonardo in mind, and realize that the person we hold up as the ultimate genius became so because he worked at it. Leonardo was very proud of the fact that he was self-educated, and he used to purposely sign himself as a "Disciple of Experience."

Let's take a look at the multiple intelligences, and see how Leonardo fared in each one.

Leonardo was astonishingly creative. He created immortal works of art, sculpture and countless other original ideas. In addition to his artistic skills, Leonardo was also an exceptionally accomplished musician. If you gave him any stringed musical instrument, even one that he had not seen before, he could very quickly "work it out" and play both known and original music on it. Leonardo was known for exuding a deep self-confidence. He loved his own company, and cared for and looked after himself as only a best friend or lover would. He was also very skilled in social intelligence: he was the most popular guest at all the parties and social gatherings in Florence. He was masterful at playing the fool, could mesmerize audiences with his storytelling, and used his vast musical ability to entertain his fellow guests – spontaneously composing and playing songs while they stood amazed.

Leonardo's fascination and love of nature and the natural, living world is well known. He considered nature to be a manifestation of God, and was exceptionally kind to animals. The story was often told how he would go into the marketplace, buy a cage of birds (they were sold either for their song or to be eaten) and in full view set all the birds free, watching with enchantment their flight patterns as they soared ecstatically in their new found freedom.

The assumption that someone cannot be both intelligent and strong is completely refuted by Leonardo. He was known for his extraordinary stamina and energy, and had a reputation as the strongest man in Florence. He was also incredibly attractive. The historian Vasari reported that Leonardo's poise was so perfect, his movement so sublime, and his appearance so astonishingly beautiful, that people would line the streets of Florence simply to see him walk to his workshop. He was like a modern-day sex god.

Leonardo particularly developed his sensual intelligence (obviously very important to an artist), and he used to exhort those around him to develop all of their senses too. He developed his visual powers to such an extent that at times his observations bordered on the miraculous. It is reported that he was the first person to see, with his naked eye, the moons of the planet Jupiter, and in his Codex on the Flight of Birds, he recorded details which remained unconfirmed until the invention of photography 350 years later proved him to be right!

Numbers were a natural part of the harmony of the universe for Leonardo. He used numbers as a basic thinking tool for measuring and calculating in all his fields of activity – art, design, engineering and invention. Pouring forth from Leonardo's unbelievably prolific mind were new designs for aqueducts, locks and dams for rivers; inventions for underwater craft and for flying machines; and hundreds of more genius engineering ideas that had never been thought of before.

Because he had studied so many fields of activity, Leonardo's vocabulary was many times greater than the average. Because of his massive imagination, he was able to combine the two to produce the most beautiful musings and descriptions. Many of his literary notes are portraits created not with paint but with words.

Leonardo is the ideal model for you as you read through *Head First*. Bear in mind that he was a child, just like everyone else, who had the fortune and ability to tune into his own intelligences, and literally, to put his Head First.

THE CHAPTERS

Head First is designed to be stimulating, informative, effective, and fun. Each chapter comprises:

1 An expanded **definition** of the intelligence, giving you a clear picture of each of your amazing intelligences.

2 A precise statement of the **benefits** you can achieve by applying the knowledge in the chapter.

3 A real life example of an **Intelligence Star** who is an ideal example of the intelligence being discussed in the chapter.

4 **Amazing facts**. In each chapter there are boxed items of information that will prove to you that you are smarter than you think!

5 **Case studies**. In addition to the main Intelligence Star example, you will discover compact examples of other individuals who have exemplified this intelligence. These examples can help you to choose some roles models as you develop your own growing brain power.

6 **Brain Workouts**. At the end of each chapter, when you are mentally "warmed up" you are invited for a Brain Workout. Here you will be given exercises specifically designed to make you smarter.

7 Self-development **Questionnaires/Tests**. Near the end of each chapter you will find a Self-development Test. These are designed to entertain and amuse you, while giving you a guideline as to what a super genius in that intelligence would answer. If you get over 50 per cent in your first attempt, you are doing extremely well. As you develop each of your intelligences, try repeating the tests, and watch how your scores rise!

In addition *Head First* contains:

**Mind Maps®. Mind Maps® are colorful, spatial learning tools that I have spent my life developing. They are brilliant route-maps for the memory, allowing you to organize facts and thoughts in such a way that the brain's

natural way of working is engaged right from the start. This means that remembering and recalling the information later is far more easy and reliable than when using traditional note-taking techniques.

In each chapter you will be given some ideas for you to construct a Mind Map® around. As well as encouraging you to develop your own, there is a complete section of color plates showing examples. (There are full details on how exactly to draw Mind Maps® in Chapter 1.)

*A Multiple Intelligence Progress Chart. At the end of *Head First* you will find your Multiple Intelligence Progress Chart. As you complete the questionnaires for each chapter, fill in your score in the appropriate section. By the time you have finished *Head First* you will have a complete "Intelligence Profile," which will give you an immediate picture of your strengths, areas needing improvement, and balances within your Multi-Intelligent Brain. Every so often you can repeat the tests, checking your progress in each different intelligence, to see how they grow over the months.

What you should be aiming at when working your way through *Head First* is a balance. It is fine to concentrate mainly on those intelligences you regard as your weaker ones, but don't forget your stronger ones and neglect them – or vice versa! Although each intelligence is linked to all the others, so when you consciously develop one, you subconsciously improve the others too, it is best to actively and deliberately work on each intelligence in turn.

While reading *Head First*, think of each of your Multiple Intelligences as a finger on a pair of unbelievably adept and agile piano-playing hands. It is possible of course for you to play your life's music with one finger, or with two: for example using only your Verbal and Numerical Intelligences, or only your Physical and Sensual ones. The music of your life, however, is far better played with all the fingers of your Multiple Intelligences performing their magic on the keyboard of your existence.

The Creative and Emotional Intelligences have been badly overlooked and often ill defined. In Part 1 I explore how you can develop the vast power of your Creative Intelligence through the amazing technique of Mind Mapping®. Moreover, you will discover that Emotional Intelligence is not one single intelligence but three – Personal, Social and Spiritual – all vitally important and all individual, separate intelligences! By the time you have completed Part 1 your creative powers will have grown considerably through the use of Mind Maps®, and you will be able to relate to yourself, to others and to the world around you with a much deeper understanding than before.

the creative and emotional intelligences

create yourself

your creative intelligence

YOUR CREATIVE INTELLIGENCE - A DEFINITION

Your Creative Intelligence is your ability to think in new ways – to be original, and, where necessary, "stand apart from the crowd." Your Creative Intelligence includes:

- **Fluency** – the speed and ease with which you can "rattle off" new and creative ideas.
- **Flexibility** – your ability to see things from different angles, to consider things from the opposite point of view, to take old concepts and rearrange them in new ways, and to reverse preexisting ideas. It also includes your ability to use all your senses in the creation of new ideas.
- **Originality** – this is at the heart of all creative thinking, and represents your ability to produce ideas that are unique, unusual, and "eccentric" (i.e.,

away from the center!) Although many people think such a person is "uncontrolled", exactly the opposite is true: originality often results from a great deal of *directed* intellectual energy, and it generally shows a capacity for high levels of concentration.

- **Expanding on ideas** – the creative thinker is able to build on, develop, embroider, embellish and generally elaborate and expand upon ideas.

Creative people usually show a lot of determination and persistence, they are often in trouble with authority, have high levels of energy when involved in their creative tasks, have a flair for life, and are often considered to be "colorful characters." They are usually interested in all kinds of music, writing and art, and often in sports and physical activity.

WHAT'S IN IT FOR YOU?

By the time you emerge from the Brain Workout, you will have greatly expanded your creative thinking ability; you will have learned, in a few minutes, how to draw (*and* that you are a quite competent artist); and the principles behind telling good jokes! In addition I will have provided you with exercises for keeping your "Creativity Muscle" in shape.

DID YOU KNOW?

The number of ideas it is possible for *your* brain to create is greater than the number of atoms in the known universe?

Whereas the traditional Numerical and Verbal Intelligences (of which more in chapters 8 and 10) tend to focus on a more analytical, logical thought process,

Creative Intelligence refers to the more explosive and dynamic thought process that leads into new realms of thinking and expression. And, as with all the other intelligences you are about to explore, Creative Intelligence *can* be taught – and it is fun!

A CREATIVE INTELLIGENCE STAR

Our first Intelligence Star is someone who definitely did not breeze through school, as you might have expected – he was severely dyslexic and struggled both through books and his academic career, being so embarrassed by his inability in reading that he spent hours memorizing texts word-for-word whenever he knew he would have to read in public. His IQ scores were low and to his teachers he was obviously not bright.

The young lad's name was Richard Branson, and the development of his Creative Intelligence guaranteed that his future would be very bright indeed!

How did he get from the unpromising position he was in as a child, to be the mastermind behind over 150 enterprises that carry the Virgin® name, with a personal wealth estimated to be approximately four and a half billion dollars?

What the IQ test had failed to measure was his burning ambition, which drove him on to find creative solutions no matter what the problems were, and to keep persisting where others would have given up long before. Those tests also never identified his ability to share his creative visions and dreams with others, and to blend their dreams with his.

As a teenager, Richard Branson became increasingly frustrated (as all creative people do!) with the rigidity of school rules and regulations. His first act of creative rebellion was to start his own student newspaper.

A dyslexic starting a newspaper?

Yes!

The original way in which Branson directed his newspaper was this: instead of focusing it on the schools, he decided to take the opposite view and focus on the students. Rather than be a standard fuddy-duddy and boring "rag," Richard wanted his newspaper to be colorful and exciting, appealing to everyone, and especially to the major corporations who would buy advertising!

Again Branson decided to "break the mold" by having not just student journalists, but by inviting rock musicians, movie celebrities, politicians, creative "names" and sports stars to contribute.

Richard and his co-editor friend Johnnie Gems did not, however, start penniless. They had £4 to help cover postage and telephone expenses, donated by his mother! The two boys worked in the Bransons' basement and scrimped and saved wherever possible – though not on their grand creative dream, which remained their driving force.

Prophetically Richard Branson's school principal (who was also obviously beginning to recognize that the IQ tests may have been wrong), said to him one day: "Congratulations, Branson. I predict that you will either go to jail or become a millionaire."

From that time on Branson expanded on his original idea, spinning off new companies, creating new products, devising new ideas and continually appealing to the dreams of others. His flagship company, Virgin Airlines, is a perfect example of creativity in action. Instead of getting caught in the normal downward spiral of chopping fares and cutting service, he again decided to reverse normal thinking, by maintaining fares but *improving* service, which included such strikingly original ideas as in-flight massages, ice-cream with movies, showers and exercise facilities.

Richard Branson himself, known as a flamboyant, colorful and extraordinarily creative human being, attributes his success to both his ability to generate and follow great creative visions, and his ability to recognize the same in others and to have them all, as a team, follow their dreams.

DID YOU KNOW?

Thomas Edison, one of the greatest geniuses of all time, who patented over 1,000 different inventions, was expelled from school when he was 12.

As you begin this chapter, it is important to re-emphasize to yourself that creativity is not simply painting a picture or playing a musical instrument. Of course, it *is* those things, but creativity is *also* cooking your evening meal, coming up with an answer to a problem at work, planning your vacation, rearranging or designing your yard, fixing up your home, or figuring out ways in which your baseball team can beat the opposition.

Now let's move on to developing your creative skills even further.

case study

Parents are among the most creative people ever to live. Apart from creating babies, they have to *create* household design; *create* breakfasts, lunches and dinners; *create* plans for vacations; *create* events and entertainments for guests and visitors; and *create* excuses for their partners and children! In a very real and most important sense of the phrase, they are literally *creating* the future.

LEONARDO DA VINCI'S CREATIVE INTELLIGENCE PRINCIPLES

That creative genius, Leonardo da Vinci, said that there were four main things he had done, and that others needed to do, in order to create a truly creative brain:

1   Develop your senses
2   Study the art of science
3   Study the science of art
4   Realize that, in some way, everything connects to everything else

1. Develop your Senses

Leonardo was recognizing, 500 years ahead of his time, that Sensory Intelligence was a singular and significant element in a developed, *creative* human brain. You will cover this more fully in Chapter 6, "Making Sense of Your Senses."

2. Study the Art of Science

It is interesting to note that Leonardo did not say simply "study science"; he said, "study the *art* of science." By this he was suggesting that science was not the dull, gray, nerdy, colorless and boring subject it is often considered to be in our modern (and in this instance, misinformed) age. Da Vinci correctly realized that all science included the "right-brain" skills of Spatial Intelligence, Imagination, Rhythm, Color and Form.

3. Study the Science of Art

This initially sounds contradictory, doesn't it: the science of art?!

Once again, however, Leonardo was correct. Art is not, as the vast majority of people believe, some "soft," wishy-washy, emotional form of personal expression or psychoanalysis. It is, as you will discover in your Brain Workout, a very exact and precise *science*.

4. Realize that, in Some Way, Everything Connects with Everything Else

Leonardo had discovered (400 years before the great psychologist William James realized its incredible significance in the structure, formation and development of human thought), the principle that, not only is your brain an association machine, it is an association machine of *infinite* capacity. Think for a moment before reading on, about the implications of what da Vinci had discovered, and about what you have just read. It will change forever the way you think about thinking, the way you think about yourself, the way you think about others, and the way you think about the nature and potential of human intelligence.

In addition to Leonardo's four Creative Intelligence Principles, there is another principle which you should be aware of: creativity, by its very nature, implies *getting away from the norm*.

The statistical concept of the norm, *the average*, gives rise to our concept of "normal." Normal is that to which your brain has become accustomed; that which gives you no surprises; that which remains the same; that which no longer shocks, startles, surprises or provokes you; that which does not stretch your imagination.

To *create* means virtually the opposite: to bring into existence something new; to give rise to; to establish an association that has never been established before.

case study

The Beatles were a supreme example of a group multiple intelligence working at genius level. They were constantly able to link together concepts that had never been linked before, and were able to produce album after album of extraordinarily new and original work. They were also renowned for their witty, playful, energetic and "far-from-the-norm" behavior – all characteristics of the creative mind. (It is also important to note that The Beatles were not an immediate success – they used their incredible persistence to try again and again and again, being rejected by more than 30 record companies before finally signing a deal.) It is hardly surprising that John Lennon, often considered the most creative of the four, should be remembered by his most famous composition: *Imagine*.

Creativity is a "by definition" awareness:

- **If Alexander the Great** had fought his battles in the way that all the people before had fought them, he would neither have survived nor would we have ever heard of him.

- **If Beethoven** had composed music in exactly the same style as Haydn, he would now be noted as a minor composer, not a giant among giants.

- **If Elizabeth I of England** had accepted the normal restrictions society placed upon women at that time, she would never have become one of the greatest rulers England has ever seen.

- **If Picasso** had only painted like van Gogh, he would have been considered simply as a copyist and irrelevant to the history of art, rather than a towering presence in the pantheon of artistic genius.

- **If** the greatest athlete of the 20th century, **Mohammed Ali**, had boxed like the average boxer, he would, literally, have been knocked out of our consciousnesses!

Now that you are armed with Leonardo's four principles of Creative Intelligence, and with a knowledge of that essential characteristic of all the great creative geniuses – removing themselves from the norm – you are ready for an incredibly exciting and stimulating Brain Workout.

BRAIN WORKOUT – DEVELOPING YOUR CREATIVE INTELLIGENCE

Improving your Creative Intelligence is one of the easiest, most fun and enjoyable tasks you will ever have!

1. Day-Dream on!

No matter what anyone may have said to you, day-dreaming is essential to your creative brain. It is necessary to your survival and should be indulged in *at least* 10 times a day. Einstein always recommended day-dreaming to his students – he himself used to imagine himself travelling from our sun, at the speed of light to the ends of the universe, exploring as he went. This imaginary journey actually gave him the final clues he needed to realize that the shape of our universe was curved and not endlessly straight as it was previously supposed.

Rather than thinking of it as a problem or a failure in your ability to concentrate, concentrate *on* day-dreaming. Use your day-dreams to hone your

DID YOU KNOW?

Day-dreaming gives needed rest to those parts of your brain which have been doing analytical and repetitive work, exercises your projective and imaginative thinking, and gives you a necessary chance to integrate your thoughts and to create.

powers of imagination, to heighten the texture and colors in your mind's eye, to improve and empower your memory, and to improve your ability to tell stories, to write and to entrance other people's imaginations.

2. Night-Dream On!

Make a point of "holding yourself quiet" just as you are waking up in the morning. See if you can catch a dream! When you do, make a note of it. Dreams are when your brain plays on the giant stage it has available to it – your imagination. In night-dreaming your brain hatches the most incredible plots, arranges the most extraordinary scenery, and creates the most astounding creatures and events. If you note down and talk about your night-dreams, you will be feeding your creative imagination with the best possible diet! All great artists, poets, writers and musicians use their dreams as a source of inspiration.

3. Note Down Your Night-Dreams

Research has shown that keeping a little journal of whatever dreams you can remember, gently gets you more in touch with the creative core of your unconscious mind. People who are in tune with their unconscious selves tend to become more relaxed, happier, and more in touch with themselves, and, of course, more creative. (This is also a good exercise for developing your Personal Intelligence – of which more in the next chapter.)

4. The Creativity Game

What follows is a Creativity Game that will open your mind to worlds you never would have thought existed for you.

On the next page write down, in exactly two minutes, and as fast as you can, every single use you can think of for a paper clip. Finish the exercise, and then check your results.

_____

_____

_____

_____

_____

_____

_____

_____

_____

_____

The scores on this test range from 0 (and this is with effort!) through 4–5, which is the global average, to 8, which is "good brain-stormer" level, to 12 (exceptional and rare), and finally to 16+ – the Thomas Edison level! The **"creativity curve"** illustrates this well. If you give someone as long as they wish to complete the test, they will average 20–30 uses.

Conventional wisdom considers this test as _reliable_: this means that your score will not change much over time. Bearing in mind that we have already seen that your brain can create an infinite number of ideas, doesn't something strike you as a little _odd_ here?!

To work out what is wrong, imagine a Brain Salesman who is trying to convince an audience that they must "buy brains." He tells them that he has the most amazing product in the universe, and that he has a number of pieces of information about it, any one of which will immediately make them want to buy. First, he explains that each brain is a super bio-computer and has a million million super bio-computer chips.

Second, he explains that the number of patterns of intelligence his product can make is the number one followed by ten-and-a-half kilometers of noughts.

Third, he points out that his product can remember virtually anything as long as it uses special memory techniques. These techniques, he points out, prove that the product can link any object with any object; for if it could not, these systems, which have worked for centuries, would immediately fail.

Fourth, he explains that his superb product can think, speak multiple languages, solve mathematical problems, see, hear, smell, taste, touch and operate a body magnificently.

Finally he reaches the climax of his presentation, and informs his audience that this amazing product can think of four or five uses for a paper clip in a minute, and 25 in a lifetime!

There is something *seriously* wrong both with the way we have been trained to think, and with the test as a true measure of your creative potential!

Further Examination of the Creativity Test

Go back to your answers and circle the one you think is your most creative idea. When you have chosen it, jot down the reasons that made you choose it. You chose it because it was the most ... what?

Now check the following list of words, and mark the ones you think best define an idea that is creative:

- Normal
- Original

- Practical
- Removed from the norm
- Bland
- Exciting

The obvious answers are that creative ideas need to be *original* and *removed from the norm*, and as such they are usually *exciting*.

If you come up, for example, with the creative idea that you could use a coat hanger to hang coats on, no one is going to beat a path to your door! However, if you thought of using it to form a sculpture or to make a musical instrument, people will be far more interested not only in your ideas, but in you.

case study

The multiple World Ice Dancing Champions, Jane Torville and Christopher Dean, were so creative that they transformed a sport and changed the way that many people listened to classical music forever. By using new and imaginative styles of clothing, never-before-seen movements and lifts, and by pushing all the then-current approaches to ice-skating to their limits, Torville and Dean were able to evoke images of Spain, Spanish dance and bull-fighting that left audiences in stunned silence and the judges wide-eyed and amazed. Many people still see Torville and Dean in their imaginations whenever they listen to the music they danced to – Ravel's *Bolero*.

Looking Again at the Creativity Test

Let's look again at the question: "Think of every possible use you can for a paper clip."

The more rigidly taught mind will assume that "uses" refer to the standard, ordinary, sensible applications for a paper clip. That same rigidly taught mind will also assume that the paper clip is of a standard size and is made of standard material. Standard, standard, standard = normal, normal, normal thinking. And normal thinking is average.

What is the Creativity Test trying to measure? Thoughts that are *removed* from the norm.

The Creatively Intelligent, and therefore more flexible-minded, will see far more opportunities for creative interpretations of the question, and so will generate both *more* ideas, and ideas which are of higher *quality*. The creative mind will expand the meaning of the word "uses" to include the phrase "connections with." Such a mind will also realize that the paper clip could be of any size, made of any material, and be transformed into any shape.

The creative mind will therefore break all the ordinary boundaries, and will include in the list of uses many "far out" (away from the norm!) applications – such as "melting a five-ton metal paper clip and pouring it into a giant mold to make the hull of a boat."

Back to your Brain Workout!

5. Learn to Draw!

You can't?

You can! What's more, you are about to do so!

A good way to start is to use Conni Gordon's introductory method of instantaneously proving to you that you *can* be an artist. Do the following Conni Gordon exercise, realizing that it can be varied many times simply by changing the shape of the mountains, changing the height of the horizon, changing the shape and number of branches and leaves of the tree, etc.

The Conni Gordon Four-Step Method®

Before you start, take a few minutes to draw a simple landscape, consisting of sky, hills, a tree and a lake.

Now, here is Conni's method for drawing the same landscape.

STEP 1 - OUTLINE

Draw a large, rectangular box and put a dot in the centre. Halfway between the dot and the bottom of the box, draw a horizontal line. Between this line and the dot, add in a slanted, uneven range of hills.

STEP 2 - SUPPORT

The white paper can support the sky area. Lightly shade in lines to delineate the hills, and use more pressure to draw water lines in the lake. Don't completely fill in the area of the lake with these lines.

STEP 3 - FORM

Freely sketch in uneven bushes along the bottom of the hills along the lake shore. Draw an "S"-shaped tree trunk from the top to the bottom of the box and fill it in. Add shorter, tapering "Y"-shaped branches to the trunk.

STEP 4 - DETAILS

Roughly scribble three separate, uneven, dark curved leaf-shapes across the tree. Add more branches to connect them up, and then fill in the bottom ground area solidly with curved grass and weed areas.

That was easy, wasn't it!

6. If you Haven't Already, Learn to Tell Jokes!

Many people fail in this art because they concentrate too much on trying to remember the words, and fail to realize that jokes are basically children of the imagination and your brain's ability to make new and surprising associations.

To make the task easy, start with "one-liners." These put little stress on your memory, give you immediate positive feedback, and are like positive electric jolts in the brains of those you entertain and amuse.

To exercise your "humour muscle" more generally, make a regular habit of reading cartoons, reading witty sayings or stories and sharing amusing anecdotes with your friends.

Read the following short jokes and analyze just what it is about them that so pleases the brain. Select your favorites to pass *creatively* on!

What did the wit call his pet zebra?
Spot

Why do lions have fur coats?
They'd look silly in overcoats

When are sheep like ink?
When they're in a pen

A group of chess enthusiasts checked into a hotel and were standing in the lobby discussing their recent tournament victories. After about an hour, the manager came out of the office and asked them to disperse. "But why?" they asked, as they moved off. "Because," he said, "I can't stand chess nuts boasting in an open foyer."

What is green, has two legs and a trunk?
A seasick tourist!

What is brought to the table and cut, but never eaten?
A pack of cards

Two Eskimos sitting in a kayak were chilly, so they decided to build a fire. But when they lit the fire in the craft, it sank – proving once and for all that: you can't have your kayak and heat it, too.

7. Play the "Everything Connects to Everything Else" Game

If what Leonardo said is true (and so far no one has proven him wrong) then no matter what two objects you take, you should be able to find a number of connections between them.

Start yourself off by noting, in the space provided, as many connections/similarities as you can think of between the two *apparently* unconnected concepts: **FROG/SPACESHIP**. (Turn to page **33** for some creative suggestions supplied by the author's students.)

Play this game regularly as a Creative Intelligence Mental Muscle development technique. A good way to do this is to simply dip randomly into your dictionary or thesaurus every day – at the same time you will be improving your vocabulary (see page **197**).

DID YOU KNOW?

At the same time as you make *mental* connections in your thoughts you are making *physical* connections within your brain? You are literally making your super bio-computer more complex, more sophisticated and more powerful.

　　The brain with which you read this now is therefore not the same as it was yesterday, and it will not be the same tomorrow!

8. Do Doodle Do!

Doodling, like day-dreaming, was once thought to be a sign of an inability to concentrate. It is in fact your irrepressible imagination forcing, no matter how hard you try to keep it down, its way out into the real world. Not only allow yourself to doodle – make it into a creative art form by expanding the variety of shapes, forms, lines and shades you use when you do doodle.

9. Apply your Creative Intelligence

Apply your Creative Intelligence to all the major areas of your life, including:

- your friendships
- all sporting activities
- cooking
- gardening
- your children
- sex

Allow yourself, as all children and geniuses do, to talk, hum, sing and laugh to yourself.

10. Write Poetry

Everyone, by nature, is a poet. Poetry, like humour, uses *association* as its major tool. Think of how love poems compare/associate the loved one's eyes with stars, limpid pools, oceans and universes; their lips with ripe fruit; their hair with golden corn or the rich black of the night; their cheeks with peaches and roses, etc.

To start, restart or continue your own poetic career, take, as you did with the Frog/Spaceship exercise, any object about which you wish to write poetry, and make imaginative and rhythmical associations with it.

Here are some examples of Edward Lear's amazing Nonsense verse to inspire you!

There was an Old Man of the Coast,
Who placidly sat on a post;
But when it was cold, he relinquished his hold,
And called for some hot buttered toast.

There was a Young Lady of Welling,
Whose praise all the world was a telling;
She played on the harp, and caught several carp,
That accomplished Young Lady of Welling.

There was an Old Man with a beard,
Who said, "It is just as I feared! –
Two Owls and a Hen, four Larks and a Wren,
Have all built their nests in my beard!"

Let your imagination go wild. Invent new words – anything that sounds right *to you*. None of it has to make any sense to anyone else. See what meaning *you* can make from seeming nonsense – don't be inhibited. Lewis Carroll was a genius at this. The little bit below, from *Through the Looking-Glass (and What Alice Found There)*, will give you a flavor of his creative imagination:

"Twas brillig, and the slithy toves
Did gyre and gimble in the wabe;
All mimsy were the borogoves,
And the mome raths outgrabe.

"Beware the Jabberwock, my son!
The jaws that bite, the claws that catch!"...

11. Play Areas

Decide in which area/s of your Creative Intelligence universe you wish to play in, and set up little areas for play in your life to encourage you to do this. For example, make it easy to go to your guitar or keyboard at odd moments; have your sketch book available most of the time; keep a note pad as a constant companion so that you can jot down thoughts, poetry and ideas as they occur to you; have music and videos that inspire your creative thinking in a place of priority on your shelves; and have your creative thoughts at or near the front of the queue in your mind. Schedule at least a few minutes per day for your creative playtime.

12. Tell and Be Told Stories

Storytelling, which is an art form you can rapidly and easily develop, is highly enjoyable for both the storyteller and the listener. Listen to stories wherever you can – they are great training grounds for your creative imagination. Interestingly, research has shown that listening to the radio is more *visually* stimulating than watching television! Why? Because in listening, for example, to a play on the radio your brain creates its own gigantic vistas, landscapes, colors and characters, exercising as it does so its Mental Muscles, rather than being spoon-fed pre-digested images from a visual screen.

The poet Ted Hughes, who helped young children develop their own Creative Intelligences by teaching them how to Mind Map® (see page **29**) and memorize in order to write poetry, was a wonderful example of someone who had trained his own creative imagination to amazingly high levels. One famous story about him is how he was once asked the apparently simple question: "What took you to Rome?" His answer enthralled his listeners for three hours!

13. Think of "Six Impossible Things Before Breakfast"

This was the famous comment of the White Queen to Alice in *Through the Looking-Glass*. Playing this great imagination game will amusingly stretch and expand your Creative Intelligence.

14. Creativity Characteristics

Research by the author and others into the field of creativity, has shown that there are 10 characteristics of behavior that identify exceptionally creative individuals.

These 10 characteristics are habits of behavior and thinking that *you* can copy to make yourself much more creative. They also provide you with an extra Creative Intelligence Brain Workout in which you can exercise and build your Creative Muscles!

Creative geniuses:

1 **Associate new and unique ideas** with the "old" ideas that already exist. Your "everything connects to everything else" game will help you with this.
2 Use **different colors** when making notes, to help them associate different ideas and to remember them. Practice and develop this aspect of yourself and you will, literally, become a more Colorful Character!
3 Use **different shapes** in Creative Thinking – again especially in note-taking. Your doodling will supplement this creative genius thinking skill for you in

your day-to-day thinking: make a habit of combining unusual elements. Joke-telling is also particularly useful in developing this aspect of your creative skills, as is the "everything connects" game.

4 **Create big internal mental landscapes** in your dreams and day-dreams, by magnifying reality and visualizing things in dramatic 3-D.

5 **Practice seeing things from different points of view.** For example, when you watch a bee land on a flower, imagine what the landing was like from the bee's point of view, or even from the flower's point of view! This Creative Thinking "Conceptual Position" game can be played with *anything* that happens in your life. (It can help enhance your Social Intelligence too, *see Chapter 3*.)

6 **Link pre-existing concepts and rearrange them** in new ways. We have already seen how Einstein's sudden creative leap of imagination led him to the realization that the universe was not, as had been thought, endless and "straight-lined," but was bounded and curved. Another example is Copernicus, who took all the then-known knowledge of the universe and rearranged it to come up with the startlingly creative realization that the sun was the centre of the solar system, and not the earth as previously thought.

7 **Reverse pre-existing concepts.** You have already seen a superb example of this in Leonardo da Vinci's Principles. He took the creative idea of "study the art of science," and by reversing it made it into the equally creative idea of "study the science of art."

   In your daily life, look for ideas that you can twist into their opposites. You will often find that they provide amazing and amusing insights.

8 **Respond fully to aesthetically appealing objects.** Embrace, with all your senses, things that are beautiful and attractive. You will find much more information on this aspect of Creative Thinking in the chapters on Sensual and Sexual Intelligences (*chapters 6 and 7*). Make a habit of focusing on at least one beautiful thing every day.

9 **Respond emotionally to all aspects of life** and the environment. The Emotional Intelligences (which we'll be covering in chapters 2, 3 and 4), are vital to the development of your creativity. Express yourself, and you'll automatically become more creative.

10 **Express themselves** in a variety of unusual and energetic ways! By the time you have finished *Head First*, you will be doing just that!

15. The Paper clip Exercise Revisited

Let's now go back and look at the paper clip exercise in the light of these creative characteristics. Remember: the average person can think of about 24 uses for a paper clip when given as long as they want. Let's try each one of the creativity characteristics and see if we can use them to generate more uses for a paper clip.

We'll keep a tally of the number of ideas we have generated as we go along.

ASSOCIATE NEW AND UNIQUE IDEAS WITH THE "OLD" IDEAS THAT ALREADY EXIST

We could use a paper clip:

1 to clip clothes to a clothes line
2 as a nose clip in an unpleasantly smelling environment
3 to clip a torn garment together
4 to clip (or seal) a small wound

USE DIFFERENT COLORS WHEN THEY ARE THINKING CREATIVELY

We could paint paper clips different colors and then use them to:

5 communicate
6 decorate a table or home
7 classify files (e.g. green = finance)
8 as colorful toys for children

USE DIFFERENT SHAPES IN CREATIVE THINKING

We could use a paper clip to:

9 make a sculpture

10 decorate an artistic design

11 signify to a friend a secret code or action

CREATE BIG INTERNAL MENTAL LANDSCAPES BY MAGNIFYING REALITY

We could use a really *BIG* paper clip:

12 as a paperweight

13 as a landmark

14 as a dam to a stream

15 as a "plank" to cross that same stream!

16 as a prop for a tree

17 as the eighth wonder of the world!

SEE THINGS FROM DIFFERENT POINTS OF VIEW

(This is a particularly useful one for this kind of creative thinking test/game.)

Seeing the paper clip from the point of view of a:

18 microbe – the giant cave which you can see in a paper clip under an
    electron microscope can be a microbe's home

19 nutritionist – you could use a chocolate paper clip as food

20 doctor – you could use the paper clip as a needle

21 musician – you could use the paper clip as a tuning fork

22 warrior – you could use the paper clip as a deadly weapon

23 philosopher – you could use the paper clip (and this exercise) as a tool in
    your search for the meaning of life

24 economist – you could use the paper clip as a form of new currency

25 itch – you could use the paper clip to scratch yourself!

LINK PRE-EXISTING CONCEPTS AND REARRANGE THEM IN NEW WAYS

(This is another particularly good one for this exercise and as a general problem solving technique.) We could use the paper clip:

26 as a writing implement

27 to pick a lock

28 in food preparation as a skewer or beater

29 for cleaning nooks and crannies (and fingernails and teeth as many people do!)

30 for adjusting the little "reset" buttons on watches, computers and other small machines

REVERSE PRE-EXISTING CONCEPTS

31 if we wanted to mess up the filing system, we could remove all the paper clips!

32 we could use one paper clip to remove another one!

It is also useful when trying to think of ideas *for* something, to think of things for which you *cannot* use it. Here are four ideas which initially seem to be *cannot* done, but when you think about them, you will find that they *can* (some suggestions are listed on page **33**):

33 you cannot fly to the moon on a paper clip

34 you cannot drink with a paper clip

35 you cannot start a car with a paper clip

36 you cannot make love with a paper clip

RESPONDED FULLY TO AESTHETICALLY APPEALING OBJECTS

We could use a paper clip:

37 as jewellery

38 as a status symbol, especially if it were made of platinum or gold

39 as a "pet clip" in the same way as people have "pet stones"

40 as a "feel nice" object for the hands, especially if it were made of some especially smooth and tactile material

RESPONDED EMOTIONALLY TO ALL ASPECTS OF LIFE AND THE ENVIRONMENT

We could use a paper clip:

41 as an imaginary friend

42 as a mood changer (red paper clips to inspire passion etc.)

43 as a reminder of some emotionally positive memory where paper clips were somehow involved...

EXPRESS THEMSELVES IN UNUSUALLY ENERGETIC AND VARIOUS WAYS

We could:

44 make an animated paper clip

45 use advanced science techniques to tap the atomic power contained within a paper clip for energy-use purposes

46 make a musical instrument from our paper clip

There! 46 uses, and it was easy wasn't it! Using the 10 creativity characteristics, see if, by using yet more different perspectives, and by thinking of things for which you cannot use a paper clip but *can*, you can get to 100. If you do you will be in the top 1 per cent of creative thinkers already.

You can use the creativity characteristics to think of solutions to problems, to play creativity games, to make up new jokes and to make your life more colorful and more fun. Enjoy doing so! This is also a fabulous game to play with your friends. Try it!

The next item in the Brain Workout uses the characteristics to help you create a note-taking tool that will vastly improve (and use) your Creative Intelligence, and will change your life!

16. Mind Maps®

Think about the first five ideas in the extended Brain Workout above (pages **11–17**), and apply them to note-taking. What kind of note-taking system would you devise to help you expand your Creative Intelligence?

Obviously, you would use one in which the links, associations and relationships between ideas were clearly shown; in which colors and different shapes were liberally used to help you clarify your ideas; and in which size and dimension were used to help you emphasize the more important ideas. You would *not* use the normal traditional linear, colorless and boring notes!

These Creative Thinking notes are called Mind Maps®, and are, literally, an easy-to-follow map of your thoughts as you create them. They are very similar to city maps, where the center represents your most important idea, the main roads leading from the center represent the main thoughts in your thinking process, the secondary roads or branches represent your secondary thoughts, and so on. Special images or shapes can represent sites of interest, or particularly interesting ideas.

Just like a road map, a Mind Map® will:

- give an overview of a large subject or area
- enable you to plan routes or to make choices, and will let you know where you are going and where you have been
- gather together large amounts of data in one place
- encourage problem-solving by allowing you to see new creative pathways
- be enjoyable to look at, read, muse over and remember.

How to Mind Map®

Mind Maps® are simple to create:

1 Use a large sheet of paper.
2 Gather together a selection of colored pens, ranging from fine nibbed ones to highlighters.

3 Select the topic, problem or subject you want to Mind Map®.

4 Get any information you will need together.

5 Start in the center of the paper with a large, unframed image which can symbolize the topic.

6 Use dimension, expression and at least three colors when drawing the central image, in order to attract attention and aid memory.

7 From the central image, radiate out key words and the most important ideas you have about the topic, each on a separate, thick line.

8 Branch thinner lines off the ends of the appropriate main lines, to show supporting data (the more important the data, the closer it should be to the central image or idea).

9 Use images wherever possible.

10 Use colors freely in your own special code to show people, topics, themes, associations or dates, and to make the Mind Map® more beautiful and more memorable.

This chapter of *Head First* was created using a Creative Thinking Mind Map® (which is shown in color plate 1), and you will find other examples of Mind Maps® throughout this book. The wonderful advantage of this thinking tool is that as well as for Creative Thinking, it can be used to help memory, review facts, general note-taking, planning and communication.

case study

Many people have found Mind Mapping® an invaluable way to help them through exams. People like Edward Hughes, who, back in 1982 was a very average student at school and got very average marks in his school tests. His father introduced him to Mind Mapping®, and Edward went on not only to achieve A grades, but also to achieve a scholarship to Cambridge University.

Decide to experiment and play with this form of Creative Thinking tool as soon as possible. You might consider doing a Creative Mind Map® on a topic such as:

- Yourself
- Your hobby
- Your ideal future
- Your best friend
- Your perfect holiday
- The planet Earth
- Sports
- Music
- This book!
- Your choice!

Your Creativity Intelligence Questionnaire follows. A score of 50 or more means that you are doing truly well. A score of 100 means that you are a genius in this intelligence. Test yourself from time to time to watch your scores rise, and enter them on the table on page **221**.

MULTIPLE INTELLIGENCE TEST – CREATIVE INTELLIGENCE

In scoring this test, give yourself 0 if the statement is absolutely and incontrovertibly untrue, and 100 if it is explosively true!

I enjoy drawing, painting, sculpting and using 3-D perspective.   SCORE ......

I enjoy dancing to the beat, distinguishing all different forms of music, playing, composing and singing.   SCORE ......

I enjoy creative writing, storytelling and poetry.   SCORE ......

I enjoy the theatre and acting, including comedy, tragedy, mime and playing the fool.   SCORE ......

I enjoy humour and regularly make people roar with laughter.   SCORE ......

People sometimes say I am crazy, mad, unpredictable, a "one off," etc. (they say it with a smile).   SCORE ......

I regularly attend shows, art exhibitions, concerts and other cultural events.   SCORE ......

I have a rich and varied dream life.   SCORE ......

I consider myself an exceptionally creative and productive individual.   SCORE ......

I am a good, creative day-dreamer!   SCORE ......

TOTAL SCORE ......

ANSWERS to the Frog/Spaceship exercise

1 They both "live" in two environments.

2 They both have launching pads.

3 They both "jump up."

4 They both land.

5 Millions of people collect them as models.

6 They both have television programs devoted to them.

7 They both have "eyes."

8 They both aim towards a goal.

9 They are both energy systems.

10 Add your own!!

"Impossible" uses for a paper clip

- You *can* fly to the moon on a paper clip – you can put it on a seat in the rocket, sit down on it, and "lift-off!"
- You *can* drink with a paper clip – you could straighten it out, drill a hole down the middle, and use it as a straw!
- You *can* start a car with a paper clip – you could use it as a fuse in the engine!
- You *can* make love with a paper clip – use your own imagination!

you and you

your personal intelligence

PERSONAL INTELLIGENCE - A DEFINITION

Many people consider Personal Intelligence to be the most important intelligence. because it concerns the only person with whom you will spend every second of your life – yourself.

This intelligence concerns self-knowledge and self-fulfillment, and is fundamentally about understanding yourself – about having a good, honest, mental model or map of yourself, and being able to learn from the basis of that knowledge. When you have a truly high Personal Intelligence you are the kind of person of whom others say "he seems to be at peace with himself" or "she seems comfortable in her own skin," and are able to overcome almost any sort of personal adversity.

Personal Intelligence can be summed up in the phrase "Know Thyself," and generally indicates that you are in charge of your reactions to events, rather than letting events control you in inappropriate and self-damaging ways. Signs that you are high in Personal Intelligence include the facts that you "know where you are going," can enjoy your own company as much as that of others, are involved in continual self-development, and are generally managing your life well. Personal Intelligence is also one of the foundation stones for the development of your Social and Spiritual Intelligences.

WHAT'S IN IT FOR YOU?

In this chapter I will show you a complete life-management approach and system. You will end your Brain Workout more aware of just how magnificent you are, with a deeper understanding of yourself, your life to date and your life in the future, with your stress reduced, and with tools to help you continue to master and increase this most important intelligence. You will also have a much greater understanding (and control) of your emotions.

DID YOU KNOW?

To make a machine that could do everything you could do – to make another you – would cost well over a *billion and a half* dollars! You are worth a lot!

A PERSONAL INTELLIGENCE STAR

Imagine that you are a Superman. Imagine that you are a healthy, successful and handsome athlete – that you are a famous actor in the prime of your life, with tens of millions of adoring fans. And imagine that one day you are galloping on horseback when suddenly a freak, sickening and nearly life-ending accident occurs. In an awful twist of fate, you are thrown from your horse and land on your head, snapping your neck in the process. In the hospital it is announced that you will be paralyzed for life, that you will never walk, swim, play, run, sail, ride or make love again.

Could you live with yourself in your new state? Could you rise above it to once again inspire the world?

Christopher Reeve has, and does. The actor who *played* Superman has, in the process of losing all his physical power, *become* Superman. In his book, called *Still Me,* he chronicles his battle to come to terms with his new life; his determination to carry on with his life – appearing on radio and TV shows and encouraging the medical world to research cures for the tens of thousands of people in similar situations to his – has inspired millions of people all over the world.

Reeve has the Personal Intelligence to know that, despite his altered physical condition, he is still himself – *still him*. He also uses his creative imagination to keep his dreams alive: that, through his Personal Intelligence and strength, the good wishes of the millions who are aware of his epic battle, and the accelerating research which he has in large part inspired, he will accomplish the "impossible" and walk again.

Christopher Reeve has been forced to cope with a huge personal crisis. Hopefully the majority of us will only have to deal with minor setbacks. However, to develop your Personal Intelligence to handle whatever fate throws at you, you must know *how* and with *what* your brain reacts.

The Car and Its Driver

A typical car-and-its-driver story will help illuminate this.

You are driving your car to work when you come to an intersection of two main roads. The intersection is controlled by traffic lights and, as you approach, the lights turn red. You dutifully stop and await the green light. As it turns green, you take your brakes off and are about to accelerate across when, hurtling across the intersection from your right, is a car traveling at at least twice the speed limit and obviously breaking the law by jumping the red light. To make matters worse, the car misses yours by only a few inches, making you very aware that you have come within a split second of serious injury, perhaps even death.

In such situations most people respond in one or a number of the following ways:

- Make an obscene gesture.
- Insult the intelligence of the driver.
- Add to the insult by adding a wide smorgasbord of expletives.
- Raise their own blood pressure, adrenaline, heart-rate and stress levels.
- Pound furiously on the horn.
- Engage in a lengthy conversation with any passengers in the car, focusing on the imbecilic nature of the other driver.
- Carry the experience on to work, explaining in righteous fury to their co-workers about the moronic nature of the driver, and expanding on the possible dire consequences.
- Store the story as a constantly-to-be-reviewed example of the irresponsibility of other members of the driving community.

Before considering the *appropriate* response, let's look at what really happened.

You were driving a little tin box you choose to label a "car." Your little tin box approached a line that theoretically stretched to infinity both to your left and right. Seeing a red dot of light hanging at an appropriate angle in the sky, you decided, based on your experience and training, to stop.

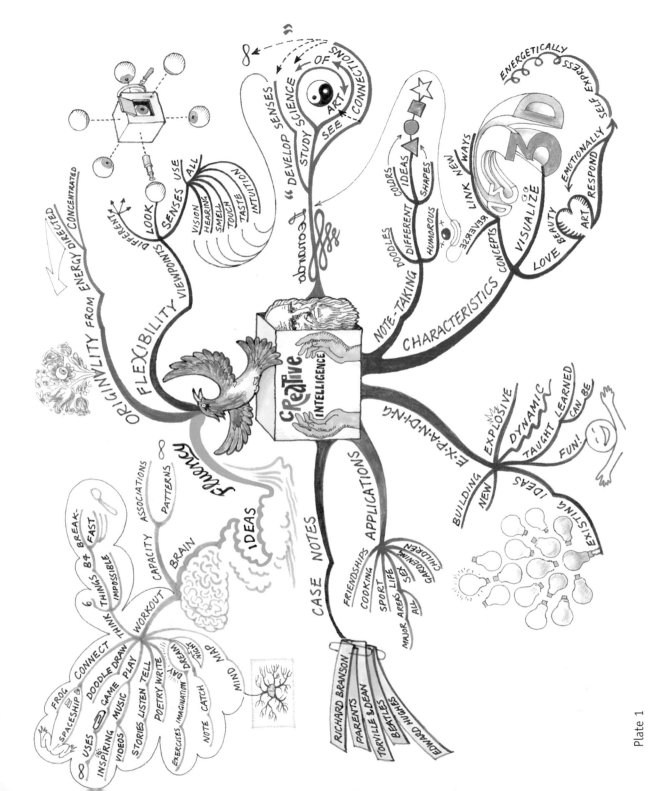

Plate 1

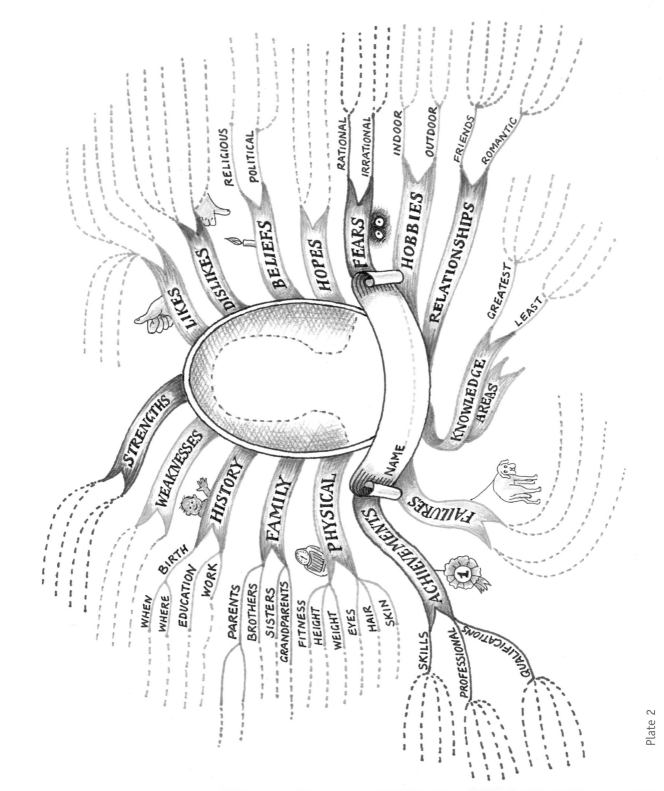

Plate 2

A few seconds later, another human being in a little tin box approached you from the right travelling at an approximately 90 degree angle to you. Seeing his similarly angled dot of red light, for some reason he decided to continue past it. His little tin box did not touch yours and disappeared off having made no contact with yours whatsoever.

It becomes quite apparent that for all the *actual* impact it has on your existence, the incident is hardly worthy of your consideration or thought!

In addition, consider the different responses to the situation you might have, had you been aware of the following possible variations to the theme. Imagine that you had known that:

- The other driver had just discovered that his wife and child were in a serious accident just down the road.
- The other driver was in the process of suffering a heart attack.
- The accelerator of the other car had become jammed to the floorboards.
- The other driver had been on a drinking binge, and was "smashed out of his mind."
- Hiding behind the other driver's seat was an escaped criminal with a gun, who had threatened to kill him if he did not drive flat-out to aid in the escape.
- The other driver was your own brother.
- etc., etc., etc.

From this you can see that our normal reactions to what happens in the environment around us are ones of emotional habit, and are usually based on an incomplete knowledge of the facts. Above all, our reactions are a matter of *choice*.

To fly into a rage when something happens is one reaction to the event, but it is not your only choice. The individual with a high Personal Intelligence will perform the proverbial "take-a-deep-breath-and-count-to-10" routine, consider the possible options, and then choose the most appropriate and positive response.

The same understanding can be used when dealing with difficult colleagues, building friendships on the basis of understanding rather than aggression and possible hurt, dealing with any situations in which you feel "provoked" to anger, and in helping your children similarly to understand their own justified and unjustified angers and the management of them.

The individual who has not developed this Personal Intelligence will spend a lot of time and energy being the "victim" of circumstance and the helpless pawn of his or her major negative thinking habit.

The choice is yours – literally.

case study

Mohammed Ali, *the* sportsman of the 20th century, had tremendous personal belief. His faith in himself as "the Greatest" not only sustained *him* during his boxing bouts – it undermined his opponents because *they* believed it too! Now suffering from Parkinson's disease, he still has that self-belief, and flatly refuses to regard himself as a victim of his body's failings.

"I am happy and content," he said, when interviewed once. "Think of all the opportunities I have had; all that I have been given. This Parkinson's disease is simply another fight. Don't worry about me, I'm okay."

The realistic person with a high Personal Intelligence is one who would commonly be known as a positive thinker. It is important to point out that this does *not* mean going about with an inane grin, claiming that everything is wonderful! It means taking each situation, no matter how bad it might be, and finding the best option for dealing with it.

Perhaps one of the best examples of this was demonstrated in a radio interview with elderly veterans of the First World War.

The War Veteran's Story

An interviewer was asking war veterans about their experiences, and had focused on nothing but the horrors of war. Many of his interviewees had succumbed to his gloom, and revealed the long-held resentments they felt and the lifetime problems that had been caused by their experiences.

One interviewee, however, a 96-year-old, was singularly upbeat, and explained that the war, unpleasant and horrifying as it was, had actually taught him a lot.

Exasperated, the interviewer finally said: "But surely, and I hope that this won't embarrass you if I explain to our listeners your physical condition, you cannot accept what happened to you with equanimity. I must tell our listeners that I am talking to you knowing that, and seeing the evidence that, during the course of the war you lost the sight in one eye, had your left hand irreparably damaged, and lost your right leg. Surely this must have had a traumatic and negative impact on your entire life?"

To which the feisty and magnificent nonagenarian replied: "Well, young man, life's a bit like that. You come on to this glorious planet with a body that has all kinds of bits attached to it. And as you go through life you might lose a bit here and then lose a bit there. But it doesn't really matter if you still have your brain alive, friends to care for and who care for you, and a mission in life to make others' lives more happy, does it?"

96-year-old Personal Genius 1 – negative interviewer 0!

Nor does being Personally Intelligent mean that you can never express fury, anger or grief. On the contrary – it means that you have *full* freedom to express these emotions, knowing that in certain situations they are completely appropriate and healthy expressions of your feelings, although recognizing that in many other situations they are not.

You will by now be increasingly aware of the fact that Personal Intelligence is a major constituent of what has been popularly labelled "Emotional Intelligence."

You should also be aware of the fact that if you develop your *Personal*

Intelligence you will similarly be improving your *Social* Intelligence, while also exercising and improving your Creative Intelligence.

And now, on to amazing new research about *your* brain, *your* skills, and how *you* can use them to manage *your* life successfully.

DID YOU KNOW?

You have a million, million brain cells, 167 times the number of people on the planet! Each brain cell is more powerful than a standard personal computer.

LEFT BRAIN, RIGHT BRAIN – AND OTHER NEW DISCOVERIES

American psychologist Roger Sperry's work on the two sides of the brain won him a Nobel prize. He and his co-researchers discovered that the left side of your brain deals generally with the following mental areas:

* words
* logic
* numbers
* sequence
* linearity
* analysis
* lists.

In contrast, the right side of your brain deals generally with the following, different mental activities:

- rhythm
- spatial awareness
- holistic awareness
- imagination
- day-dreaming
- color
- dimension.

Sperry also discovered that while the left side of your brain is active, the right side goes into a relaxed, semi-meditative alpha-wave hum. When the situation is reversed, and the right side of your brain is active, the left side of the brain goes into the same relaxed, semi-meditative alpha-wave hum.

Subsequent experiments have shown that virtually everyone has the full range of mental capabilities. Unfortunately, due to miseducation and misinformation, most of us tend to think of ourselves as innately skilled in only a few of these areas (which we regard as usually concentrated in either the left or the right side brain activities, but rarely across both), and inherently unskilled in the others. We compound the problem by assuming that our weaker areas are forever unobtainable. However, a more accurate self-description would be, "I have developed *these* areas of my potential ability, while for various reasons I have left *those* areas dormant for the time being."

As a result of Sperry's research, millions of individuals have started to train the incorrectly labelled "weaker" aspects of their mental abilities. They have found that those "weaker" skills, when nurtured under the direction of the right teachers, are capable of blossoming, regardless of age. They have also found that these newly developed skills feed back into previously developed skills, expanding existing skills even further.

DID YOU KNOW?

The great geniuses of history – leading scientists and artists such as Einstein and Picasso – were not in fact dominant in only one side of the brain's activities, but were enormously wide-ranging in their interests and activities. The great scientists often came across their breakthrough ideas while day-dreaming, and most of the great artists and musicians were incredibly organized and analytical, especially in relation to their work.

Each one of us *needs* this balance between the left and right sides of the brain. If this is not achieved we become relatively ineffective. In other words, in any self-management and Multiple Intelligence-development system, it is essential to make sure that the two sides of your brain are actively balanced.

Left-brain, Right-brain Check

Even after hearing the evidence, many people still doubt that they *really* have both left-brain and right-brain abilities. To check on your left brain, simply ask yourself whether or not you can speak and understand one language. You can? Then the left side of your brain is already operating in a far more sophisticated way than the most modern computer. In order to have learned that language, you must have used the other left-brain skills of numeracy, logic, analysis and sequencing too.

To check on your right brain, ask yourself the question: "Where am I when I come up with those bursts of imaginative, creative, problem-solving ideas?"

Most people find themselves thinking up such ideas in the bath (remember Archimedes!), taking a shower, in bed, driving, or walking in the countryside or by the sea. In these relaxed and unhurried situations the individual is at ease, and usually alone. When you have such imaginative ideas, it is the right side of your brain that is functioning. And it functions best in situations like those described, during which time the left side of your brain gets a well-earned rest!

However, it is now time for your Brain Workout!

BRAIN WORKOUT – DEVELOPING YOUR PERSONAL INTELLIGENCE

1. Self-talk

Monitor those constant little conversations that go on in your head between you and yourself. Check to see whether they are positive or negative; whether they add to the general quality, health and happiness of your life, or whether they subtract from it; whether they coach you well with encouragement, or whether they deflate your self-image and demotivate you. Adjust them appropriately. Design yourself a great brain cheer-leading team!

2. Treat Yourself as Your Best Friend

You should be! Take time for, and to be with, yourself. Only when you are truly happy with yourself can any other relationships be developed properly. Be aware that being happy with yourself *now* will naturally include wanting to improve constantly – it is your brain's natural desire to continue to learn and to grow throughout your life.

Learn to treat yourself as affectionately as you would treat anyone who was especially dear to you. You can use all your other intelligences to do this, especially your Sensual Intelligence (*see Chapter 6*). Pampering yourself can include such wide-ranging activities as having a massage; taking yourself to a special restaurant; giving yourself a special vacation; setting aside some uninterrupted "quality time" to read a book you've been wanting to for ages; taking a bath in special oils; buying that item of clothing that *feels* so good; realizing a sexual fantasy; etc. Make a mini-Mind Map® showing all the ways you *could* pamper yourself, and act on it!

3. Continue to Develop your Other Multiple Intelligences

Each of your intelligences will help you develop your relationship with yourself and will make you more confident and at ease. Ideas that may help stimulate your thinking about your self-development include:

- Instruments to play.
- Board game skills to acquire.
- Riding or driving skills to acquire.
- Books to read.
- Questions to explore.
- Knowledge to gain.
- Facts and data to record and remember.
- Films and theater shows to see.
- Ideas to develop.
- Jokes to remember and the skill for telling them.
- Languages to learn.
- Music to listen to, learn about, and become expert in.
- Logical debating and arguing skills to acquire.
- Mechanical and physical skills to develop.
- Emotional and social skills to enhance.

Divide your self-development into sub-divisions, and avoid the tendency to become overenthusiastic. *Don't try to become Leonardo da Vinci in a day!* Give yourself a reasonable number of self-development goals to begin with, and build on them only when your initial skills are acquired and your initial goals are achieved.

4. Wait!

In explosively emotional situations, give yourself a brief moment to pause and contemplate your options and responses. Is it necessary or appropriate to "blow your top?"

5. Take Regular Breaks

These allow your brain to "change gear" and to find momentary resting states and mental oases in the normal hustle and bustle of the day. During such times your brain has a chance to integrate and contemplate, giving you the feeling of being a still "eye" in the middle of the daily storm.

case study

The Dalai Lama is a shining example of someone with a high Personal Intelligence. He fled the occupation of Tibet by China, and now leads a government-in-exile in India. His continued fight for his country's independence, and advocacy of non-violence and compassion have touched people from all walks of life, and have won him the Nobel Peace prize. Despite his heavy responsibilities and work schedule, he spends much of his time thinking and meditating, and is renowned for his incredible aura of inner peace.

6. Express your Emotions

Express your feelings of affection, love and appreciation more regularly to those around you. Use your Creative Intelligence to discover how many different ways, some of them very simple, there are of doing this. For example, thank people *whenever* it is appropriate; tell people you love them more often than you currently do; use emotional words such as "feel" rather than "think"; allow yourself to cry; and, especially when you are happy, express your feelings both with your words and your body.

7. Be Honest with Yourself

Although this may sometimes be painful, certainly in the initial stages, your brain is a truth-seeking mechanism, and will always reward you in the long term for telling the truth – especially about and to yourself. Telling the truth also puts considerably less stress and strain on your memory!

8. Explore the Arts of Meditation, Auto-suggestion and Self-hypnosis

These arts have been developed over many thousands of years by most of the world's major societies. They are all variations on the same theme, which is the development of self-knowledge and inner peace by regular moments of deep relaxation and contemplation. These moments can be as simple as taking five minutes out to sit quietly and empty your mind of all the incessant thoughts, worries and "noise" that go on inside our heads. Or else you could try "alternate nostril breathing" – breathing in through one nostril and out of the other! This makes you concentrate on breathing slowly and deeply, which not only relaxes you but has the additional advantage of getting more oxygen to your brain! No one system is the "best." Choose the one that most fits your needs and desires at the particular moment.

9. Gather Moments of Contentment

As you go through your day, watch out for "moments of contentment": the smile on a child's face; a cup of tea or coffee at just the right temperature; a bird singing; a friend calling unexpectedly – whatever small things give *you* a moment of pleasure. When such moments occur, take a mental "snapshot" of them and store them in your memory for future review and ongoing pleasure.

10. Silence

Promise yourself at least 10 minutes of silence per day, giving your brain a break from its normal non-stop activity. Many of the great geniuses did this – you won't be surprised to learn that Leonardo was a champion at it! Doctors have found that giving yourself these mini-breaks is one of the best ways of improving health and reducing stress, and they are especially useful to all those people struggling to juggle demanding jobs, family life and social responsibilities.

During these moments of silence and tranquillity, your brain *will* sort out priorities, and refresh and invigorate itself for the next round of activity. Mind Maps® are wonderful tools to use with your "time-outs." When everything seems to be conspiring against you, and you are "fire-fighting" everywhere, the Mind Map® allows you to see things in perspective, to prioritize appropriately and then to act on those priorities.

YOUR COMPLETE SELF-ANALYSIS AND MANAGEMENT GUIDE

Take Control of Your Own Life

Those who have taken a conscious decision to do this have been found to live longer and healthier lives. It has also been discovered that it is a major boost to your survival chances in situations such as serious accidents, imprisonment and life-threatening illnesses.

case study

Solo yachtsmen, by definition, take control of their own destinies. If anything goes wrong during a race, they are totally alone on the waters. British solo round-the-world yachtsman Tony Bullimore was trapped for four days in his capsized boat in the freezing Antarctic ocean, while competing in a race around the southern tip of Australia. His boat ran into 70 mph winds and was overturned by 40-foot high seas. When rescuers finally reached his boat, Bullimore was still strong enough to free himself from the upside-down cabin and swim underneath the boat to safety, in 0°C water.

The Dream Hobby

Most people have a "dream hobby" – that hobby they have always dreamed of taking up, but which they have put off either through "lack of talent" or insufficient time. These dream hobbies, the stuff of which day-dreams are made, are an *essential* part of our nature. The most popular and universal ones include:

- painting
- playing a musical instrument
- becoming a popular entertainer
- travelling
- flying
- gliding
- diving
- sculpting
- craft work
- becoming a top athlete or sportsperson.

These dream hobbies are *not* idle fantasies, but are those "untended" parts of us, begging us to pay more attention.

A "Dream" Self-development Technique – Allowing for Serendipity

Serendipitous happenings – those spontaneous, unorganized, out-of-the-blue experiences that sometimes happen to us – are a *necessary* part of our lives. The problem with many self-development systems is that their assumptions are left-brain dominant and leave no space for such serendipitous happenings. As a result life becomes monotonous, rigid, "colorless" and routine.

Any well-balanced personal management system *must* include the opportunity for such freewheeling time. This could include leaving certain days, weeks or even months totally open for you to do whatever you want: sleeping all day, or drifting away on your own, or working your guts out on some project, or visiting friends, or completing a major life goal – *whatever* you feel like at the time, with no previous planning allowed.

Similarly, if you *have* carefully orchestrated and organized your life, and if some completely unexpected event throws all your careful planning into a momentary shambles, don't get stressed about the disruption: wait until things begin to settle down and then allow your *flexible* management system to take up the slack.

As an example of how delightful and memorable such serendipitous moments can be, a friend of mine on a highly organized business trip to Scandinavia had an eight o'clock breakfast-plus-business meeting cancelled unexpectedly. This left my friend at a loose end for a few hours. She ended up wandering through parks and by the seashore for the entire morning, relishing the totally free time and space she had to let her mind drift and play. She spent one of the most peaceful and memorable mornings of her life – a window of freedom in an otherwise rigidly regimented existence had suddenly been opened to her.

Life and our intuition often offer such gifts. Rather than struggling against them, learn to accept and enjoy them.

One common example of where such serendipitous happenings can occur is the airport! If by any chance you do get involved in long delays, be prepared to take advantage of this unexpected opportunity. Take along fantasy-enhancing books, games that you can either play by yourself or with friends, magazines or articles you have been waiting for the time "to get around to," sketch pads, puzzle/game books, etc. When you incorporate "Serendipitous Awareness" into your life, you will often find that you are *wanting* your flights to be delayed!

"Chunking," Self-development and the Need for Love

Recent findings about your brain add three key functions to the "engine room" of your Life Management Programme:

1 The ability of your mind to "chunk" – to organize things in packages; as when you categorize things into their appropriate compartments, and when you try to associate items you are attempting to remember.

2 The need for a co-ordinated programme of self-development, including general self-management, physical health and vocabulary improvement.

3 The necessity for love in all its various forms, both giving and receiving.

Armed with all this new information about your brain and its amazing capabilities, you are now ready for a series of special and exciting self-analysis and development games and exercises!

SELF-EXPLORATION ACTIVITIES

You are about to begin a series of activities that will enable you to analyze, monitor and change your life. As you will see, the way in which you have used, are using and will use your brain intricately relates to each exercise. Spend as much time as you like (general guidelines will be given) and make sure you do the exercises in the order given, completing each one before moving on to the next.

The exercises are fun to do and will benefit you for a lifetime. Using your own insights, you will answer such often-asked questions as, "How come nothing seems to work out right?" "What's the matter with me?" and "Isn't there more to life than *this*?" You will be able to look forward to a life that is more in tune with who you really are and what you really want for yourself and for your family and friends. No longer will your future be one in which events, and other people, dominate you.

Your self-development path has many exciting twists and turns, many delightful surprises, and some hard truths. You will find answers to such fundamental questions about yourself as:

- What have I done?
- Who am I?
- What do I want to do?
- Who do I really wish to become?

The process of your self-examination, though simple to describe, is by no means always easy to do, and very often, when looking truthfully into your "self-mirror," you'll want to say, "That isn't me." Persevere.

Obituary Writer

Imagine that you have the opportunity to write your own obituary. Try it, being as honest as possible.

Some people need perhaps half-an-hour to two hours for this exercise; some prefer to mull over the obituary and the implications of their life-to-date for as long as two days to a week. Keep the length of your obituary to between one and four pages.

If you found that your obituary was satisfactory to you, then you have a solid foundation on which to build your future. If you found that you would have liked your life to have been more interesting and exciting, or you would have liked to have contributed more to the human race to date, the remaining exercises will help you to make the appropriate adjustments, and to set goals that are more in tune with your ideals.

Your Self-analysis – The "I-Am" Mind Map®

This exercise, which should take you at least an hour, and may take as long as a day, involves using both the left and right sides of your brain to examine *who you are now*.

Using a large sheet of paper (an artist's pad is ideal), you are going to do an "I-Am" Mind Map® of the various aspects that make up you at this moment in time. A Mind Map® uses the various elements of your left and right brains in order to give you an externalized map-picture of your thoughts on any subject – in this case your thoughts on you. There are more details about Mind Mapping® on pages **29–30**, and before you do this exercise have a look at the example "I-Am" Mind Map®, color plate 2.

In the center of your large blank white sheet, draw a *compact* image of either yourself or something that you feel represents yourself. Then, using as many pictures, images and key words as possible, develop a *complete* picture of yourself, with the key words branching off from the center, and the secondary words branching off from the key words, and so on – much like the branches and twigs of a growing tree.

Areas that you must cover in *detail* in the self-analysis include:

- background
- strengths
- weaknesses
- hobbies
- accomplishments
- failures
- likes
- dislikes
- physical self-description
- family
- beliefs
- areas of greatest knowledge
- areas of greatest ignorance.

Throughout this exercise the definitions, extensions and meanings of the words are as *you* interpret them. For example, under "Strengths" you might include "frankness," whereas another person might include the same quality as a

"Weakness" under "blunt!" Be as honest and detailed as you possibly can.

If your Self-analysis exercise has been as honest and detailed as it should be, you may have already confronted some of those "hard truths" I mentioned. Remember that it is in those areas that you will be able to make the greatest improvements.

Your "To Do" Mind Map®

Take another large sheet and note down in *detail* the things that you have to do. This should include:

- all the telephone calls you have to make
- letters you have to write
- people you have to talk to
- washing
- cleaning
- shopping
- cooking
- caring for others
- tasks you have to accomplish
- social and business events you have to attend
- projects you have to complete and desks you have to clear
- files you have to update
- things you have to review
- books you have to read
- subscriptions you have to make or cancel
- financial affairs you have to straighten out
- people you have to apologize to
- anniversaries and birthdays you have to remember
- etc.

In addition to these detailed areas, include more general areas, such as habits you want to change, long-term goals, etc.

Make sure that this Mind Map® is exhaustive. The first burst of ideas may take between half-an-hour and an hour to put down, but other items may pop up from time to time before you move on to the final exercise, "Your Ideal Future." Give yourself a maximum of two days to do this. You may find it useful to look at the Time Juggler Mind Map®, color plate 3.

Remember, one of the "to dos" is occasionally to "not do" – to allow right-brain breaks and serendipity! Encourage your right-brain/Multiple Intelligence agenda!

Your "To Do" Mind Map® may look daunting. Don't worry. You will find it more manageable once you have got the idea of "chunking" (see page **51**).

Your Ideal Future

Let your right brain go! Imagine that you have limitless time, resources and energy, and that you can do *anything* that you wish, for all eternity. Again, using a large sheet of blank paper, and having a compact image in the center that pictures, for you, the essence of your Ideal Future, develop a Mind Map® (or ten!) on all those things you would like to accomplish if there were no limits placed upon your imagination and capacity. This Mind Map® should include all those dream hobbies that have been waiting for expression, as well as any other dreams you may have had for yourself.

Spend at least an hour on this exercise and use as much of your right-brain color and imagination as possible. This section should include all your secret "if only ..." desires. It should also include those things you *really* would like to do: a number of people jot down "seducing the entire population of the opposite sex," but when they examine whether they would really want to do this, find (often to their surprise), that they don't!

Your Personal Intelligence Questionnaire follows. Remember, a score of 50 per cent or more means that you are truly doing well. A score of 100 per cent means that you are a genius in this intelligence. Check yourself over time to watch your scores rise and enter them on the table on page **221.**

MULTIPLE INTELLIGENCE TEST – PERSONAL INTELLIGENCE

In scoring this test, give yourself 0 if the statement is absolutely untrue, and 100 if it is explosively true.

I am truly self-confident, self-knowing and content.   SCORE ......

I am able to express appropriate emotions, and do.   SCORE ......

My attitude to life is realistically, fundamentally and overridingly
positive.   SCORE ......

I am a happy, enthusiastic and energetic person.   SCORE ......

I am in control of my own life and of my responses to the
situations that occur in it.   SCORE ......

I enjoy time on my own and am seldom bored.   SCORE ......

I feel my life is in balance and harmony. If it should get out of
balance I know how to bring it back.   SCORE ......

I know I have the necessary willpower and discipline to change or
create a habit as I wish.   SCORE ......

In communication, my body language is always consistent with
my message, and I regularly use varied and open-armed gestures.   SCORE ......

TOTAL SCORE ......

NOTES

you and them

your social intelligence

SOCIAL INTELLIGENCE - A DEFINITION

Social Intelligence refers to your ability to use all your other intelligences to relate in a positive way to those most complex of all creatures – other human beings! Social Intelligence applies to your one-on-one meetings, to small and large group meetings, and to your ability (in this modern age), to deal successfully with the media, if and when you need to.

When you are socially intelligent, you understand and appreciate the very differing personalities you meet, as well as what motivates them, what their personal needs are, and how you as an individual can make them comfortable and pleased to be with you.

Professor Howard Gardner of Harvard University, author of *Multiple Intelligences*, said that if he had to choose the most important of the intelligences, he would vote for Social Intelligence. Why? Because getting on with other people is so critical to our survival and success.

What's more, as we discover more and more about what an amazing and amazingly complex organism the human being is, then the ability to deal with one or more of them must itself be an extraordinary ability and one of extreme significance.

WHAT'S IN IT FOR YOU?

In this chapter I will show you how to develop your vital Social Intelligence. You will become more confident, have a much more active and successful social life, will become a far better communicator and fearless public speaker, and will greatly increase your social horizons.

A SOCIAL INTELLIGENCE STAR

Can you imagine spending 27 years in prison, living those years in horrific squalor and semi-isolation, and then emerging to become one of the world's greatest leaders?

This is what Nelson Mandela did.

Emerging, literally, into the light after nearly three decades of living in dank cells, Mandela exhibited a Social Intelligence that has rarely been equalled. He would leave prison and go on to:

- Lead rallies of over 100,000 people, who watched him in awe and who felt completely embraced by his personality.
- Meet one-on-one with Heads of States ranging from dictatorships, through Communist empires to democratically governed countries. Each one would

invariably proclaim Mandela to be one of the most entertaining, engaging and charming people they had ever met.

- Play with poverty-stricken black children in Soweto and have them squealing with delight.
- Deal for days on end with the editors of multi national newspapers and magazines, the vast majority of whom wrote glowing reviews on this "extraordinary man."
- Deal with rebellious revolutionary groups, who nearly always came round to Mandela's interpretation of the social situation.
- Address thousands of teachers, emphasizing to them the importance of education and of their role in it.
- Lead giant crowds of sports fans in cheering for national and international teams.
- Address billions of people world-wide on global television networks, always on issues that were deeply at the heart of improving Social Intelligence, and the subsequent improvement of social relationships on a global basis.
- Finally, and most remarkably of all, display no bitterness whatsoever in public for his years of persecution.

On the basis of all this, Nelson Mandela was awarded the Nobel Peace prize.

It is important to realize early on that a fully developed Social Intelligence will enable you to relate one-on-one with a wide variety of other people. It will also enable you to relate successfully to all sorts of different groups – small or large. On the next page, rank your Top Social Communicators of the last century and, more importantly, note down next to each name key words or phrases that support your nomination.

Who?   Why?

_____   _____

_____   _____

_____   _____

_____   _____

_____   _____

What are the skills and characteristics that your Top Communicators share? List
them here:

_____

_____

_____

_____

AN INTELLIGENCE THAT GIVES RISE TO FEAR?

How do you feel about speaking in front of a group of people? If you are like
many, many others you won't be too keen on the idea!

DID YOU KNOW?

The number one fear for humans – greater than the fear of snakes, spiders, mice,
insects and creepy crawlies, war, famine, disease, alien attacks and death – is fear of
public speaking!

In fact, fear of public speaking scored *twice as highly* as the next most common fear in a recent survey.

At first glance this seems like a surprising result, but on deeper investigation it can be seen as a very rational and quite predictable response. Many people have had little or no training in presentation skills and speaking in public, and often, especially in work situations, find that they are suddenly expected to give a presentation to their co-workers, or clients or to their manager, the outcome of which can have a siqnificant effect on their current and future careers. Even during social occasions (especially important ones like weddings), where the speaker has got friends around for moral support, speechmaking can be a very stressful experience if people are not prepared.

No wonder the natural response is fear!

Fear not!

Having read *Head First* and developed your Multiple Intelligences – including your Social Intelligence – you will feel more confident and relaxed during such occasions, and will automatically make your audience feel the same. The thing to remember is that communicating to a large group of people is really the same as communicating to one other person. This should help you feel less oppressed by numbers, and relate to everybody more personally.

To check the truth of this, think about yourself at a theater or at a concert, and think about your own relationship with the people on the stage. All the while you are listening and watching, surrounded as you may be by hundreds of others, you are the only one listening with *your* ears and seeing with *your* eyes; you are the only one reacting physically and emotionally to the performers as *you* do; *you* are the only one who will remember the show in the way in which *you* will. The relationship, therefore, between the performers and you is entirely a *personal* one, regardless of whether you are on your own, with one other person, or with one million people.

The great geniuses of Social Intelligence understand this and react appropriately. You can too.

Another tip to remember when making any sort of speech in public, which will help you relax and allow your natural intelligence shine through, is to *prepare* your material *thoroughly*. It may seem rather obvious, but if you know what you are going to talk about, you will be able to take control of the occasion. (Look at the Best Man's Speech Mind Map®, color plate 12, for an example of how to plan and prepare thoroughly.)

case study

The top television chat-show host Oprah Winfrey is brilliant at "triple-tasking" with her Social Intelligence. She can make an individual feel completely comfortable and at ease in front of a 100-person studio audience, while at the same time involving and entertaining 10 million viewers.

The individual with high Social Intelligence skills also deeply understands the unique nature of every individual.

case study

The greatest military leaders were often renowned for their interpersonal skills. Alexander the Great was famous for establishing an extraordinary camaraderie with his men. He would share their hardships with them, fight with them at the front of the battle lines, incur wounds as they did and compare scars with them. After battle, no matter how tired he was, he would visit all his soldiers and listen to their tales about their own dangers and heroic deeds during the fight. Because he was one of them, his soldiers followed him to the ends of the earth.

Because our modern society has created so many classifications and "–isms," we have often fallen into the trap of thinking that nationalities, colors, language groups and political and religious groups were somehow "all the same." Nothing could be further from the truth!

To demonstrate for yourself just how unique you and every individual surrounding you is (and thus to immediately raise your Social Intelligence), play the following word or brain-association game with your family, friends and co-workers. It will give you a deeper understanding of yourself, of the nature of understanding and *mis*understanding, and of the infinitely variable individuality of those around you.

THE BRAIN-ASSOCIATION GAME

Your first task is to write down, as fast as you can, the first 10 key words that come into your head when you think of the concept of "head."

Your next task is to find three friends, and give each of them a blank piece of paper. Ask them to do exactly the same exercise as you have just done. Make sure that none of them sees or knows what words the others have written down.

When all four of you have completed your first "private" 10 key words, compare them. Look first for any words that are common to all four of you, then any words that are common to any three and then any words that are common to any two of you. A common word means one that is absolutely identical – the spelling must be the same; even plurals count as different words. Therefore, if you had put down the word "coin" and one of your friends had the word "coins," these would not be considered the same, because they are not spelled the same, and they have fundamentally different meanings.

When psychologists were asked to predict the results of this game, they assumed that there would be four or five words in common. However, the results are astoundingly different!

In any group of four it is very rare to get even *one* word that is common to all members of the group. A few groups of four find a word in common to any three of them, and the majority of groups find at least one word that is common to any given two members. Most significantly for the student of Multiple Intelligences, an overwhelming majority of the words generated by the members of a group are unique!

When groups who had achieved the dizzying heights of one common word among all four of them, were asked to do the same exercise on that common word, the results were the same as with the original word: even that which was thought to be common contained within it the seeds of difference. Knowing that each human brain contains trillions of bits of information, you can now add to this the knowledge that each one of those trillions of centers of meaning is unique to that individual.

DID YOU KNOW?

Since the beginning of time, there have been 70 billion people – each one astonishingly different from all the others.

Now you know how completely unique you are, and how completely unique everyone else is, you can see just how precious and valuable each and every other person is. This knowledge should help you raise your Social Intelligence. How? By making you more open, sensitive to and interested in the extraordinary combination of intelligences and experiences that shine out to you from every face you will ever meet.

THE NEED FOR FRIENDSHIP AND LOVE

Human beings are social creatures, and recent studies have shown that one of the basic requirements people need to survive is love and affection, in all their many forms – brotherly, spiritual and sexual.

To help you realize how important love is for you, think how you feel when love has been taken away from you: you will probably find either a tendency towards tremendous and immediate hurt, pain and despair, or an opposite reaction towards a steel-hard defense/aggression. Both indicate the importance of this basic human need.

You might be wondering why love should be included in a book on the development of Multiple Intelligences based on the latest brain research. Love is included because your brain, not your heart, is the center of your emotions, and if it is satisfied in the area of love, most other aspects of your self-management and development will automatically slot neatly into place.

An example of how a knowledge of your brain and the operating of Personal and Social Intelligences (including the concept of life-management) weave nicely together and can be found on many people's doorsteps!

In this typical situation, a man or a woman who has been working all day using the predominantly left-brain activities of reading, writing, analyzing, thinking and talking, comes home. His or her partner at home has also been working, but in a more right-brain mode: cooking, ironing, shopping and cleaning. While all the business person wants to do is collapse into a chair with a drink and to give his or her left brain a good rest, the partner wants to talk, exchange ideas, and exercise the left brain, while giving the right brain a rest. The result all too often is a row, with one accusing the other of pestering and nagging, and one accusing the other of being uncommunicative and inconsiderate!

Such situations can often lead to the complete breakdown of a relationship, whereas a simple understanding of the way in which the two parties' brains are operating would help diminish the danger.

In situations like the one described above, having a "Buffer Zone" – a time between your actual physical meeting and your mental getting-together – is the ideal solution. It allows each of you the time and space for your brains to settle down and become more balanced.

Now that you know just how important Social Intelligence is, how to overcome any fear of it, how important friendship and love are, and just how amazing and interesting you and all your fellow human beings are, you are ready for your next Brain Workout.

BRAIN WORKOUT – DEVELOPING YOUR SOCIAL INTELLIGENCE

Your Social Intelligence is one of your most flexible intelligences, and is one of the most rewarding, easy and enjoyable to develop.

This Brain Workout is divided into strategies designed to help you improve your social intelligence when meeting people for the first time, for relating to those you know, and finally for ending relationships.

Beginning Relationships

1. Remain Constantly Aware of What a Miracle You and Others Are

This will automatically open up your interest in others and thereby your senses. Others, sensing your appreciation of and interest in them, will automatically become more open to and interested in you, and so the positive loops of your relationships with others will grow.

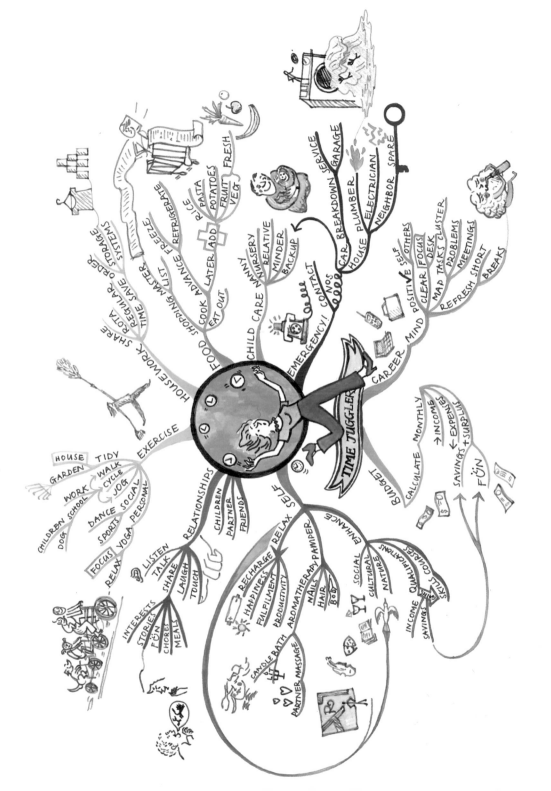

Plate 3

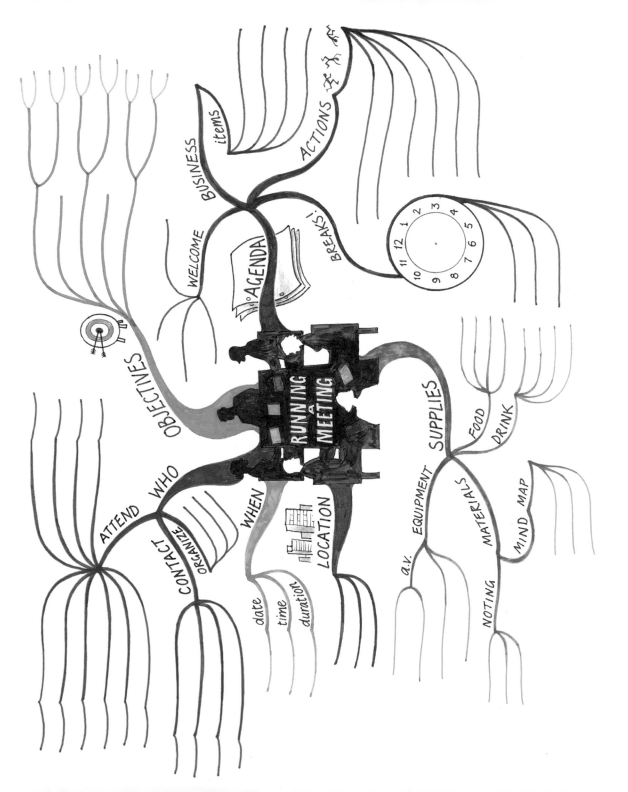

Plate 4

2. Attend Shows and Plays

Theater provides you with a stage on which multiple interpersonal relationships are acted out and often commented upon. The theater is therefore a wonderful training ground for you to expand your appreciation of the multiplicity of human relationships, and to incorporate that understanding into your own life. Another good idea is to watch videos/films of the best classic masterpieces.

DID YOU KNOW?

A playwright is a superb example of a person with a developed Social Intelligence, for in order to write (or to act) in a play, you must literally "get into the skin" of all the various characters portrayed. This is why Shakespeare is considered to be England's (if not the world's!) genius of literary geniuses.

3. Play Around with Questions

The Zen question, "Who learns more in a conversation between a wise man and a fool?," is a very useful one to think about!

4. Learn From the Greats

Look over the list you made earlier of your greatest communicators (page **64**), and make a Mind Map® of their common skills. Decide to develop these skills, one at a time, for yourself.

5. Expand your Social Horizons

Set yourself the goal of experiencing a wide variety of different social occasions, including festivals, mega-concerts, dances and celebrations of all sorts. Visit other cultures and explore other religions, always taking the role of the "Eager

Student", asking to be shown and instructed what to do and how to behave most appropriately on those different occasions. People love to show and share their special knowledge with others, and as they do so you will both learn and rapidly develop your Social Intelligence.

6. Collect People's Stories

From the youngest to the oldest, everyone has a "favorite story" – the tale of some unusual, extraordinary, terrifying or magnificent thing that uniquely happened to them. Ask them for that story, or stories. What is the most amazing thing they have ever done? What was the funniest thing that they ever experienced? Had they at some time nearly died? Have they ever fought in a war? What was the most ridiculous/stupid thing they ever did?

Ask them to tell their tale. Then *you* tell them *yours*!

7. Take a Presentation Skills Course

Such a course will encourage you to be your magnificent self, and will give you the opportunity to use many of your other intelligences, especially your Verbal, Sensory, Spatial and Creative Intelligences.

8. Dress to Impress

Make sure that your presentation of yourself in general appeals to the senses and intelligences of others. Your clothes are of particular importance in this context – just think of your reaction to people based on the cleanliness, colors, textures, "tailoredness" and suitability of their clothes. Many studies have been done on "Power Dressing," and they all confirm that in one important way, *"Clothes maketh the man ..."* For the next few days study the effect that other people's dress has on you, and also the effect it seems to have on the wearers themselves. You will come up with some remarkable findings!

Being in Relationships

9. Learn to Listen Twice as Much as you Talk

Always remember that you have *two* ears and *one* mouth! People will often compliment the person with a high Social Intelligence on the wonderful conversations they have had together. Very often these conversations were predominantly monologues on the part of the person doing the complimenting! The ability to ask the right questions and to listen to the answers with care and interest are critical social and learning skills.

One good way to make conversation, especially if you are shy, or afraid of running out of ideas yourself, is to ask people questions about themselves. For example, if you are thinking of taking a vacation, ask them if they have any ideas; if you are interested in cooking, find out if they are and get some original thoughts from them; if you are interested in sports, then probe their interest. Always look for common ground. When you find it, the conversation will flow naturally and spontaneously.

10. Make a Habit of Always Finding Good in Others

Always try to approach people thinking the best of them. This will start all relationships on a positive note, and will increase the probability that the other person will then open up to you, and find positive qualities in you. This upwardly traveling spiral will continue. However, the opposite is also true. Beware!

11. Discover the Uniqueness of Others

When you wish to understand more deeply those close to you at home or at work, do the brain-association exercise (page **67**). Place the important key concept of the moment (it could revolve around such ideas as "love," "teamwork," "romance," any "-ism," "fairness," etc.) in the center of a page. Each person then independently writes down the first 10 words they can think of in connection to the central concept. When you have all done this, work on bringing your understanding of each other into closer alignment.

12. Getting What you Want/Need from Others

Those who can get what they need or want from other people (*without* bullying or threatening them into it!) are definitely Socially Intelligent. Here are some tools to help you:

* Be honest.
* Make sure that you have a good reason for wanting it.
* Make sure there is some benefit for the person in giving it to you.
* Go in with a positive attitude – not arrogantly, but confidently expecting success.
* Ask with a smile. And make sure the smile is real!

These tools for getting what you want and need can be applied to asking for a raise, applying for a job, requesting "add ons" for items you buy, getting extra or "difficult" orders from a restaurant or hotel, and certainly to your sex life.

13. Dealing with Conflict

To develop this Social Intelligence skill, go back to the advice to listen twice as much as you talk. Most conflict is born of misunderstanding. If you allow your "opponent" to express fully the extent of the anger, pain or anguish they are feeling, the situation will already be massively diffused. In such situations you must keep a firm, though not rigid mind, and must keep your own vision (and that of the person with whom you are in conflict) firmly set on a positive outcome.

Here are some tips on dealing with those "impossible" people we all come across from time to time:

- Put yourself in their shoes, and try to find out exactly *why* they are being "impossible."
- Let them know how you feel about the situation, and see if you can come to some sort of a compromise.
- Change your thinking about them: are there circumstances which would justify their behavior, or circumstances in which *you* would behave in the same way? It is amazing how a bit of reflection helps promote tolerance!
- Reorganize your life so that they feature less in it.
- If *all* else fails, reorganize your life to avoid them altogether!

14. Managing and Leading

All great leaders have a few very simple formulas that inevitably lead them to success. Follow these tips to improve your own managing skills:

- Establish a very clear vision and goal for your team.
- Make sure that everyone is in complete agreement with the goal. If anyone is not, be willing to negotiate a plan that will meet at least some of their needs.
- Give regular rewards for successes along the way.
- Consider all the opinions in the team and then make the decision you feel is best. Stick to your decisions wherever you can.
- Regularly check your team's progress towards the goal.
- Constantly try to think of new and creative ways of achieving the goal more rapidly.
- Whenever you encounter difficulty, keep a completely positive attitude, knowing that you can go through, over or around *any* difficulty. Apply your paper clip thinking!
- Think of ways of using each one of your different intelligences to motivate your group.

It is extremely unfortunate that many managers and leaders still do not apply these principles for success, but threaten and bully their staff instead. Not only is this counter-productive – creating unwilling, demoralized and inefficient workers – it could also lead to legal action against the company and the manager concerned.

Ending Relationships

15. Ending Relationships

Ending any relationship, whether a romantic one, or one of friendship or a social/business relationship, can be one of the most painful experiences in life, especially if you are the person on the receiving end of the announcement. If you are the one doing the ending, try to put yourself in the other person's shoes, and make the message as direct and painless as possible. It is useful to concentrate on all the good aspects of the relationship: what you valued about the person's friendship, or how you appreciated their work, or what it was that made you fall in love with them in the first place. If you both concentrate on the good memories of the relationship and treasure them, you will be more likely to remain friends. Remember that your friends, lovers and co-workers all carry part of your history tied up with theirs (as you do theirs): value those moments in history when it is time to move on.

USE MIND MAPS® AS A COMMUNICATION TOOL

Most speeches and presentations are boring and dull because the method of preparing them (linear-sentences, single-color notes) is itself boring and dull! Moreover, the brain does not either listen or speak in proper sentences – it uses a more integrated approach, using images and associations.

Consider these examples of good communicators, and how they used different images to inspire their listeners:

- **John F. Kennedy,** who in his famous "Man on the Moon" speech inspired an entire nation to marshal all its resources to land a man on the moon *within 10 years*
- **The Beatles,** who used music and words to influence and change an entire generation
- **Martin Luther King,** whose "I have a dream" speech has now become *the* example of how to include rhythm and imagination in order to inspire millions and to change the way in which the world can think
- **Beethoven,** who used music as the ultimate communication device. His Ninth Symphony still radiates out a message of joy, freedom and brotherhood over two centuries after his death
- **Mohammed Ali,** who in his time communicated with more people than anyone in history before him. His message? "Don't fight, teach your children to read."

Mind Maps® "speak as the brain speaks": in colors, with images, and with associations. To see an example of this, just have a look at any of the Mind Maps® in the plate section, for example Running a Meeting (color plate 4).

You will find that, as you progress through this book, and as you think about it more deeply, the Mind Map® is a vehicle, a tool, which can help you deal with everything, and help you increase every one of your Multiple Intelligences.

Your Social Intelligence Questionnaire follows. Remember that a score of 50 per cent or more means that you are doing really well. A score of 100 per cent means that you are a genius in this intelligence. Check yourself over time to watch your scores rise and enter them on the table on page **221**.

MULTIPLE INTELLIGENCE TEST – SOCIAL INTELLIGENCE

This intelligence refers to understanding, positively relating to and communicating with others – what motivates them, their various personalities, how they function, what their perceived needs are, how you as an individual can make them comfortable, and, in short, "what makes them tick."

To check your current Social Intelligence, score yourself from 0–100, where 0 would mean that the statement is absolutely untrue and did not apply to you at all, and 100 would mean that you agreed with the statement completely and utterly. Be as honest as you can.

I listen with understanding and compassion, and am well-known for doing so.   SCORE ......

Whenever I am involved in negotiation, the result is always win/win – both sides are satisfied and think they have gained.   SCORE ......

I am able and love to lead teams of different and differing people to achieve given goals.   SCORE ......

I delight in the multiplicity of human characters, and am sensitive to all different personality types.   SCORE ......

People regularly come to me to help them gain insight. I *do* help them to gain it.   SCORE ......

I am known for my personal warmth, compassion and capacity for affection.   SCORE ......

In social gatherings I excel at helping others to relax and laugh.

SCORE ......

In conversation or in public speaking I maintain meaningful eye contact.

SCORE ......

I am able to communicate my own point of view successfully without antagonizing others. SCORE ......

I receive consistently good service in restaurants and shops. SCORE ......

TOTAL SCORE ......

heaven knows!

your spiritual intelligence

SPIRITUAL INTELLIGENCE - A DEFINITION

Spiritual Intelligence is concerned with being part of the bigger scheme of things. It involves seeing the "big picture". Spiritually Intelligent people are motivated by personal values that involve reaching beyond their own interests to those of the community at large. Such people will add to these characteristics a wisdom and understanding of themselves and of others acquired through a lifetime of experiences, a general regard and respect for humanity, a compassionate rather than aggressive attitude and a global vision (many people describe this as the acquisition of wisdom).

Spiritual Intelligence can be seen as a step on from the two intelligences we have just looked at – Personal and Social. It is a natural progression from a knowledge, appreciation and understanding of yourself, through a knowledge, appreciation and understanding of other people, to a knowledge, appreciation and understanding of other creatures and the universe. Contact with and an understanding of nature is a major aspect of Spiritual Intelligence. It is noteworthy that throughout history tribal and spiritual people – for example, Native Americans and the Aboriginal peoples of Australia – were known for their concern for the conservation and management of the environment, and for their respect for animals and nature.

Another concept of Spiritual Intelligence is "self-actualization" – the comprehensive intelligence described by American psychologist, Abraham Maslow, as the ultimate human goal in the hierarchy of needs. Maslow's research suggested that the average person needed to sort out, in the following order of importance, food; shelter; physical health; family; education and social integration; and accomplishment. When these needs are met the brain and spirit are free to explore the grander realms of the spiritual, and to become what Maslow called a "self-actualized Human Being."

WHAT'S IN IT FOR YOU?

When you have finished the Spiritual Intelligence Brain Workout, you will be in a better position to sort out your life's priorities, be refreshed, more in touch with yourself, with nature and with the universe (and climbing rapidly up the ladder of Maslow's hierarchy of needs!)

A SPIRITUAL INTELLIGENCE STAR

This intelligence star could have had the above definition of Spiritual Intelligence as a part of her own self-description. Mother Teresa was born in Albania in 1910, and went at the tender age of 18 to India to teach at a convent school in Calcutta, taking her final vows in 1937.

In 1948 Mother Teresa left the convent in order to work with the poor directly. She had seen the appalling squalor, isolation and desolation in the Calcuttan slums, and made it her mission to work there, alone, in order to bring about improvements in the people's living conditions.

Realizing the slum dwellers' desperate need for medical help, she went to Paris where she trained in medicine. Mother Teresa then returned to Calcutta and opened up some classrooms for the destitute children.

She was gradually joined by other nuns, and in 1950 founded her sisterhood – the Missionaries of Charity. Shortly afterwards her "House for the Dying" was opened, and by 1957 she had started to work with the ultimate outcasts – the lepers.

Even though in failing health, well into her 80s Mother Teresa still traveled the world giving help and compassion to others. Like other Intelligence Stars, Nelson Mandela and the Dalai Lama, she was awarded a Nobel Peace prize for her services to humanity.

case study

Another remarkable woman who served her fellow humans out of compassion for their suffering was Florence Nightingale. She endured extraordinary prejudice, the dangers of war and unbearable living conditions in order to nurse the wounded of the Crimean War. Many soldiers reportedly lived rather than died not only because of her physical caring for their injuries and wounds, but because of her unswerving faith that they would survive.

BRAIN WORKOUT - DEVELOPING YOUR SPIRITUAL INTELLIGENCE

There are many ways of developing your Spiritual Intelligence.

1. Work on your Personal Intelligence

Knowing yourself is one of the foundation stones for developing Spiritual Intelligence.

2. Develop your Social Intelligence

A deep understanding of others will burgeon into a growing and compassionate love for them.

3. Spiritual Paths

Be aware of the enormous, tempting and wonderful variety of spiritual paths. Realize as you read this that around the world, people are enjoying the benefits and wonders of many traditions – Eastern mysticism, Buddhism, Chinese Taoism, Islam, Christianity, Hinduism, Judaism, etc. If you are particularly interested in developing this aspect of your intelligence, as hundreds of millions of people are, make a study of the different religions, gathering from them the many wonderful riches that are available. Many people in the West, for example, have incorporated the Eastern practices of meditation into their own personal lives.

DID YOU KNOW?

Over three billion people – over half the population of the planet – are actively pursuing Spiritual Intelligence and knowledge.

4. Read!

Read the religious texts of the world, looking in them for stories that will help you move your own life down a more spiritual path.

There are some wonderful proverbs and sayings to be found too. Select your favorite ones and apply them regularly to your own life, while probing into their expanding universes of meaning and wisdom. Try some of the following as a starting point:

- The best things in life are free.
- A chain is no stronger than its weakest link.
- Do unto others as you would have them do unto you.
- Every man is the architect of his own fortune.
- It is not work that kills but worry.
- If you want to reach the top of the mountain you need to get rid of the weight on your back.
- Smile and the world smiles with you.

5. Study the Microcosmic and Macrocosmic Worlds

Exploring the intricate, complex and profoundly beautiful nature of the microcosmic world, as well as the vast, magnificent and beautiful nature of the macrocosmic universe, will help inspire in you the awe in creation reported by all spiritual leaders. Rediscover physics, and learn how miraculous many "everyday" things *really* are. Take time to really look at nature next time you are in a park or in the countryside. Watch and learn from nature and wildlife films. Buy a small telescope and study the stars and planets.

6. Spend Time with Nature

Spend as much time as you can outdoors in the country, or just in a nearby park. This "communing with creation" was and is reported by many geniuses and spiritual leaders to be the source of their inspirations, realizations and insights.

case study

Professor Stephen Hawking, the brilliant physicist who has been crippled by Motor Neurone disease since the 1960s, has spent his life probing the secrets and mysteries of the universe. Through his work he has become deeply interested in spiritual matters. As he explains at the end of his best-selling book, *A Brief History of Time*: *"What is the nature of the universe? What is our place in it and where did it and we come from? If we find the answer to that it will be the ultimate triumph of human reason – for then we would know the mind of God."*

7. Develop your Sense of Humor

Contrary to popular belief, spiritual individuals are *not* dour, somber and serious! People with high Spiritual Intelligence tend to have bubbling and effervescent personalities and senses of humor, delighting at the wittiness and wonders around them.

8. Develop your Childlikeness

Many leading psychologists, educationalists and spiritual leaders have said that if you wish to become spiritual and wise, you must "become as a little child again." They are correct. Don't confuse this with developing your child*ish*ness; rather, develop your child*like*ness.

The characteristics of the Spiritually Intelligent individual include many of the characteristics of a child: a wonder and awe at the mysteries and magic of the natural world; an insatiable curiosity; a natural and spontaneous generosity; an open-mindedness; and a general enthusiasm for life. These are what you should aim to develop!

9. The Good Things in Life

Make a Mind Map® of all the good things in your life. Do this properly and realize how many gifts the universe gives you. Consider things such as your senses, daylight, birdsong, friends, your heart, your hobbies, your health, etc., etc. You should be able to find as many good things in your life as you can uses for a paper clip!

10. Know your Values

Your spiritual nature is often shown by what you value. Take time to consider and then make a note of all those things, attitudes and ideals you value. Ask yourself "Why?" Make sure your actions and being reflect these values (for example, if you value "honesty" do your actions reflect this in *all* situations?).

case study

Mahatma (the name means "Great Soul") Gandhi was a spiritual leader who felt that all great global goals should be achieved by spiritual means and by non-violent opposition. His policy was to avoid bloodshed, and to fight by fasting and non-retaliation, in order to shame the perpetrators of violence into peaceful solutions. One famous example of the application of this thinking occurred when Gandhi was approached by a distraught Hindu. His son had been killed by Muslims, and in revenge he himself had killed a Muslim child. The man came to Gandhi in despair, asking him what he should now do. Gandhi considered the question, and then said: "*Go and find a Muslim child who has been orphaned by the riots between your two religions. Take that Muslim child into your own Hindu home and raise him as your own son, but as a Muslim.*"

11. Charity

Make charitable behavior a part of your life. This does not mean you have to work in a soup kitchen for hours each week, but it does mean being aware of the wider community you live in, and taking part in its life. If you have school children, go along to Parent–Teacher meetings; get involved in a local charity, volunteering to do a couple of hours work at a fund raiser, or giving things away that you don't really need. On a day-to-day level, charitable behavior can include little, simple things like giving a bit of help to a new person at work, helping a disabled person cross the street, or giving directions to someone who is lost.

12. Material Things

Many people consider material things to be the antithesis of spirituality. This is not so. The world *is* primarily a physical, material thing, as are all the component parts of it, including you! A spiritual attitude is not one that denies the existence of physical things; it is an attitude that accepts physical things as gifts, realizes that they can be both beautiful and, at the same time, temporary, and that the values attached to them are a matter of personal choice. A spiritual attitude will delight in being given things, but will delight even more in the act of giving.

13. Brain-fasting

See if there is a regular presence in your life that reduces your spiritual calm in some way. Could it be television? Could it be the regular doses of depressing news you listen to on the radio or read in your newspaper? Consider giving yourself a break from such regular irritations, and devote that time to your soul.

14. Get Rid of your Excess Baggage

In your life you will be carrying around many things, both mental and physical, that drag you down. Remember that saying before: *"If you want to reach the top of the mountain you need to get rid of the weight on your back?"* It's true!

15. Refill your Spiritual Self Daily

Discover a way to refresh your spirit, and whatever it is, *do it daily*. It may be spending time with nature; it may be a few moments of silence; it may be helping others; it may be pursuing a spiritual goal; it may be meditation. The choice is yours.

16. Mind Map® your Vision

Use the Mind Mapping® process to clarify and build your personal Vision of your own place and your mission on this planet. Make the Mind Map® as beautiful as you can. When you have completed the first draft, place it where you can see it daily. Carry a mini version of it round with you. Increasingly, make your decisions and live your life based on your Vision.

DID YOU KNOW?

It has been predicted that a movement towards greater spirituality will be one of the 10 great trends of the 21st century.

It is time for your Spiritual Intelligence Questionnaire. Remember that a score of 50 per cent or more means that you are doing very well. A score of 100 per cent means that you are a genius in this intelligence. Check yourself over a period of time to watch your scores rise, and enter them on the table on page **221**.

MULTIPLE INTELLIGENCE TEST – SPIRITUAL INTELLIGENCE

Mark your score from 0–100, where 0 would mean that the statement was absolutely untrue and did not apply to you at all, and 100 would mean that you agreed with the statement completely and utterly. (In this test, saints would score 100s, and devils would only achieve zeros!)

My life has a sense of complete and positive purpose to it. SCORE ......

I feel a great connection to, and often feel "at one" with, the universe and/or God. SCORE ......

I understand and have a deep knowledge of myself. I do what I say and I express this in my "be-ing." SCORE ......

I am known for my playful, irrepressible and bubbling sense of humor, and a childlike (but *not* childish) view of the world. SCORE ......

I am deeply at peace with myself. SCORE ......

Other life forms generate in me a sense of awe, wonder, love and respect. SCORE ......

Others consider me more mature and wiser than average. SCORE ......

I achieve the right balance of appropriate caring for others whilst staying "cool" about the outcome of such caring. SCORE ......

I enjoy "serving" all other people to the best of my ability and at every opportunity. SCORE ......

I am amazed at my capacity for wonder! SCORE ......

TOTAL SCORE ......

For hundreds of years the body has been increasingly disconnected from the brain in the way we think about intelligence. Typically, the bright individual has been thought to be physically weak; the fit individual and athlete summed up as "all brawn and no brains!" Finally, at the beginning of the 21st century we are realizing that these attitudes are not only wrong – they are the opposite of what is true.

As you will discover in Part 2, your *body* is fantastically intelligent in many ways. All the intelligences we have dealt with so far, the Creative Intelligence and the three "Emotional" Intelligences, require that your body and senses be operating to their full potential. The next three chapters will help you guarantee that they are!

PART 2

the bodily intelligences

body talk

your physical intelligence

PHYSICAL INTELLIGENCE – A DEFINITION

Your body talks. It holds regular conversations with you and with others in many different ways. Athletes solve problems or "make things" with their bodies. Dancers, actors, surgeons, and indeed everyone who uses his or her body shares this intelligence.

Your Physical or Bodily Intelligence relates very closely to two other exceptionally important intelligences: your Sensual Intelligence (which you will find out about in the next chapter) and your Spatial Intelligence (more details on this are in Chapter 9). Happily these three intelligences work very closely and symbiotically together, so that as you increase one, you will automatically be improving the others. You *can* have your cake and eat it too!

WHAT'S IN IT FOR YOU?

When you have trained yourself to be physically intelligent (and yes, it *is* a trainable intelligence), you will be physically co-ordinated, balanced and poised. You will also be aerobically fit, will be eating a generally healthy diet, and will be liberally sprinkling your exercise periods with rest periods. As you develop this intelligence, you will find yourself more able to play *all* and *any* physical sports.

The more balanced and physically fit your body becomes, the more balanced and mentally fit your brain will become. The two work in harmony. The reality is far more the case of "a healthy mind in a healthy body" than "all brawn no brains!" For example, as you increase your physical and aerobic fitness, you take in more oxygen. When you take in more oxygen, your brain immediately gets more of this tremendously valuable fuel. As a result all your mental functions improve.

A PHYSICAL INTELLIGENCE STAR

Our Physical Intelligence Star participated for 13 years at the highest professional level of his sport. It was a physically demanding one, played by big, muscular men, and requiring extraordinary agility, tremendous strength, lightning quick reactions and speed, physical resilience, long-term stamina and outstanding willpower.

In a game of giants this physically intelligent genius was a giant among them. His name? Michael "Air" Jordan, generally accepted as the greatest basketball player ever. Michael Jordan could leap so high that he seemed to "hang" in the air, contorting his body into the most fantastic shapes as he did so, in order either to avoid opponents or to creatively worm his way through to the basket. Hence "Air!"

With his Physical Intelligence in full flight for those 13 years, he established 21 National Basketball Association (NBA) records, including the highest average number of points per game (31.5), the most seasons as the league's leading scorer (10), the most seasons as the league's leading scorer of field goals (10), and the most seasons as the league's player with the highest number of field goal attempts (also 10). He also played in the gold-medal winning US Olympic teams of 1984 and 1992.

Michael Jordan, like so many other people who excel in one intelligence, has also developed his others. He was named by *Fortune* magazine as the most marketable sportsman in the world, thanks to his Creative, Social, Verbal, Numerical and Personal intelligences.

Physical Intelligence is a quality we all share. Like mathematics, we can temporarily lose it, but it can *always* be regained.

Many painful, frightening or embarrassing experiences can help us onto the wrong track in terms of our own estimation of our Physical Intelligence. Balls dropped or hitting us painfully, joints twisted, muscles pulled, coming in last, the mocking of others, all these can convince the athlete-to-be that "this is not for me."

And yet still, deep down, we love the healthy expression of our bodies in action and identify with our physical heroes and heroines. What happens when a spectacular goal is scored, or an incredible race is won, or a new and astonishing world record is established? The thousands watching will spontaneously rise in jubilation at their own dream-come-true-in-another.

Your Physical Intelligence can be trained. It consists of your overall physical fitness, your balance, agility and co-ordination, anticipation, reaction time, strength, flexibility and aerobic fitness.

In order for your body to perform well it needs to be in top condition. It's time for a Brain (and Body!) Workout.

THE BRAIN AND BODY WORKOUT – DEVELOPING YOUR PHYSICAL INTELLIGENCE

Your Brain and Body Workout is complete with exercises, illustrations, goals and examples for comprehensively improving your body's well-being and raising your Physical Intelligence.

1. Overcome your Fears

Millions of people have fears of some or all physical sports, especially those involving water (such as swimming), and heights (such as abseiling), or simply the fear of making a fool of yourself! Pick a personal major fear and decide that it is going to become part of your history!

Using all your Multiple Intelligence skills, find a good class or personal coach in that particular fear area. With their help, you will confront and overcome your fear through practice and experience, whether that fear is physical or psychological.

case study

Tiger Woods, the golfing phenomenon, has accomplished his astounding successes partly through "natural talent," but mostly through an awful lot of hard work. Woods was last afraid on a golf course when he was 11 years old and matched against a boy who was a year older. *"It's no good being intimidated on the golf course. I have a lot of belief in my own game and my own abilities. I have put in the hard work. If you don't put in the hard work, then you obviously can be intimidated because you don't know what can be accomplished. I have put in the work. I know what I can accomplish."*

2. Take Regular Exercise

Your body is *designed* to take exercise, and will benefit from it in all ways. The most difficult part is to start – once you have, the enjoyment and benefits will be so great you will become positively addicted! To help you get started, first make the decision; second, put it in your diary; third, make sure that you have the appropriate facilities or equipment (this doesn't have to be anything elaborate – a pair of good sneakers for jogging is sufficient); fourth, tell friends and hopefully get them involved as well; and finally make a Mind Map® of all the advantages it will bring you – the Mind Map® will act as a guide and temptation! You may find color plate 5 a useful example.

3. Muscular Strength

Your body is propelled and moved by its millions of muscle fibers. The stronger each of these is, the more surely and co-ordinated your movements will be.

DID YOU KNOW?

You have 200 intricately architectured bones, 500 totally co-ordinated muscles, and 7 miles of nerve fibers to move your body!

Get yourself to a gym and work on each of your major muscle groups (see the illustration overleaf).

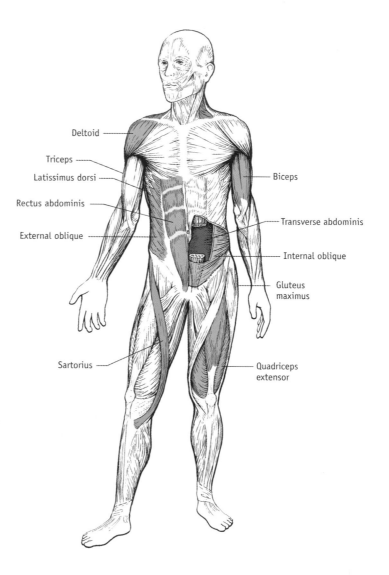

Deltoid

Triceps

Latissimus dorsi

Rectus abdominis

External oblique

Biceps

Transverse abdominis

Internal oblique

Gluteus maximus

Sartorius

Quadriceps extensor

A good way to build up muscle strength is to find a weight you can only just lift, and lift it five times. Have a minute's rest; lift it another five times; have another minute's rest; and then finish that muscle-group exercise with one more five-times repetition.

4. Flexibility

When your body is flexible, the energy can flow more freely through both your cardiovascular and your nervous systems. Flexibility is surprisingly easy to develop and maintain. There are many people well into their 80s and 90s whose limbs are as flexible as they were when they were in their 20s.

Practice stretching, either doing basic stretching exercises at home, or join a yoga or dance class, or take up one of the so-called "soft" martial arts like t'ai chi – whatever you find fun. Or get yourself to a gym.

5. Balance

Balance is crucial to your physical ability – your ability to interpret the billions of nerve impulses that come from all parts of your body, via your balance mechanisms and movement receptors, directly into your brain.

There is a simple exercise you can do to check your current balance efficiency.

Stand on your left leg, holding the ankle of your right foot behind you with your right hand, and extending your left arm forward. Hold this position for as long as you can.

Next, try the exercise standing on your right leg. Again time yourself.

The exercise is completed when you move your foot or lose your balance.

Now on to the difficult one: repeat the same exercise, both on the left and the right leg, this time with your eyes closed! This exercise particularly measures the balancing mechanism based in your inner ears. Now rank yourself according to the following table.

Eyes open balancing
- 5 minutes or more – excellent
- 4–5 minutes – very good
- 3–4 minutes – good
- 2–3 minutes – above average

- 1–2 minutes – average
- below 1 minute – your body needs balancing!

Blind test
- 40 seconds or more – excellent
- 30–40 seconds – very good
- 20–30 seconds – good
- 10–20 seconds – average
- below 10 seconds – needs work.

Repeat these simple exercises regularly, and the conversations between your body and you will vastly improve.

6. Anticipation

In all physical activity and sports, anticipation is vital. You need to be able to look, see, hear and react quickly to the flow of events. Great athletes, especially ball game players, have an almost magical quality of apparently being able to react just *before* the event – it is called "reading the game."

As with all skills, this can be developed. A good game for this is to stand in a circle of friends (between 6 and 10 of you). Use two standard sports balls (basketball, soccer, cricket, tennis, etc.) and start throwing them to each other. The minute a ball is received by one player it must be passed to another who does not hold a ball. Start this game slowly, and gradually increase the pace.

7. Agility and Co-ordination

Agility and co-ordination are a mixture of your physical and mental speed of movement. The simple game of hopscotch is a wonderful way of improving your agility and co-ordination, and can be practiced with the goal of increasing the speed with which you complete the course. Skipping with a skipping rope is also good for this, as well as increasing your aerobic fitness.

Reaction times tend to slow as people mature. This leads many to the erroneous conclusion that it is a natural part of ageing. However, the main reason for this decline is simply because the "system" is not being used.

You can test your reaction time with a simple "drop-the-ruler" test. You will need a friend to help you with this one.

Stand straight with your arm in front of you, your hand held out with your thumb and index finger parallel to the ground in an open pincer grip. Your friend holds a 12-inch ruler vertically, an inch above the space between your finger and thumb. Your friend must try to drop the ruler without giving you any clue as to when it is being released.

All you have to do is to catch it between your thumb and forefinger. The less distance the ruler falls, the faster your reaction time.

The average person catches the ruler between the six and eight inch marks, which (using the laws of gravity) gives a reaction time of between 0.177 and 0.204 seconds. Check yourself against the following table:

Inches	Reaction Time (Seconds)
5	0.161
6	0.177
6 1/2	0.184
8	0.204
8 1/2	0.210

The healthier, more alert and more aerobically fit you are, the more rapid your reaction time will be. Once again your developing intelligences help your intelligences to develop!

8. Your Brain and Aerobic Exercise

Although your brain weighs only three-and-a-half pounds, which is usually somewhere between 1 per cent and 3 per cent of your entire body weight, it consumes *20 per cent* of the oxygen intake, which provides your energy. This is because your *billions* of brain cells are constantly undergoing fantastically complex electrochemical changes as they process the enormous amount of information that constantly pours through you.

DID YOU KNOW?

Within your body there is enough atomic energy to build any of the world's greatest cities many times over.

To maintain the efficient operation of this entire system and all its Multiple Intelligences, it is important to make sure that a regular supply of fresh oxygen is provided, and one of the best ways of doing this is to embark on a basic programme of *aerobic* (oxygen supply) fitness. This can take many forms, and should involve an activity that is both interesting and personally stimulating to you, or else you will just get bored with it. The most effective aerobic activities include:

- running and jogging
- swimming
- cycling
- cross-country skiing
- dancing
- strenuous hiking or climbing
- squash
- skipping with a rope.

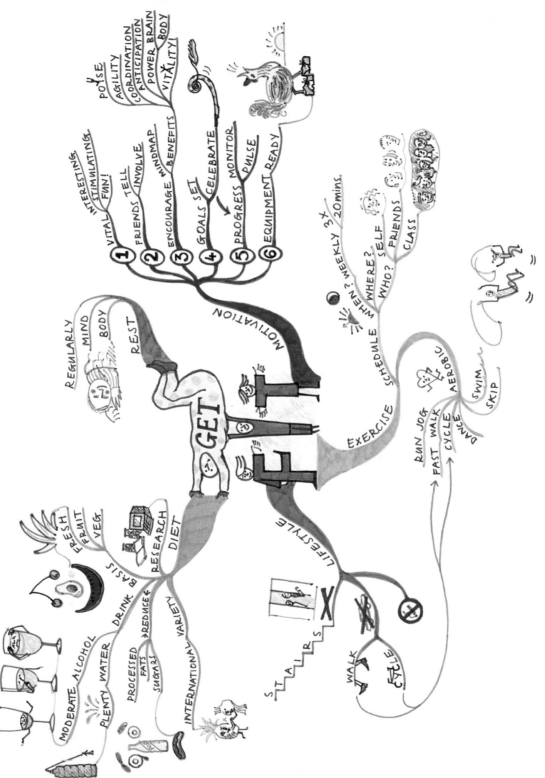

Plate 5

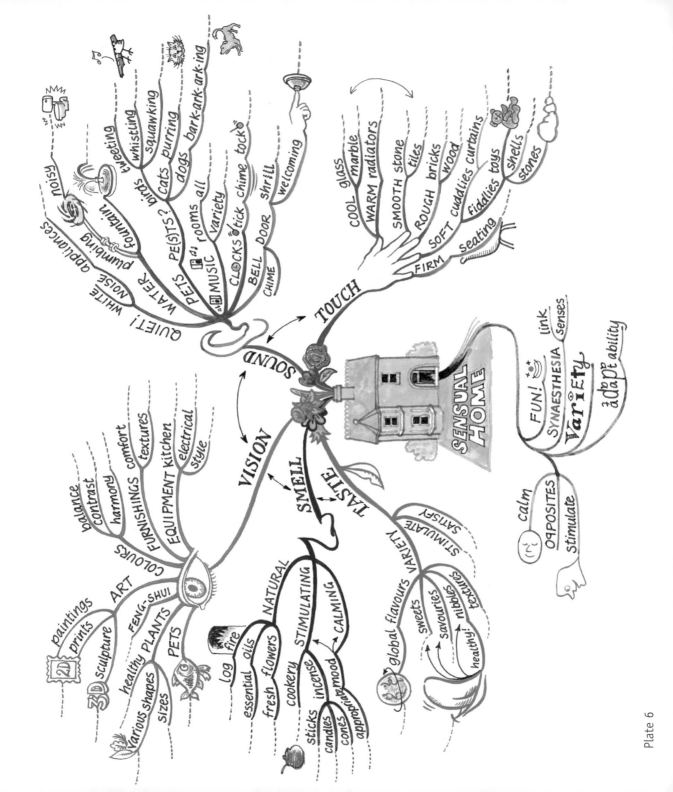

Plate 6

These are by no means the only effective aerobic exercises; any others you are familiar with that can keep your heart pumping at approximately 120+ beats a minute for twenty minutes, at least three times a week, will provide you with the "oxygen food" that you need.

DID YOU KNOW?

Your heart beats on average 36 million times *every* year, pumping 600,000 gallons of blood through 60,000 miles of arteries, veins and capillaries each year.

In addition to supplying your brain with this extra energy, you will notice that including aerobic and breathing exercises (for example, alternate nostril breathing, described in Chapter 2) into your self-development programme increases your other intelligences, reduces stress, increases stamina and leads to a general feeling of well-being.

It is a funny thing that it is precisely at the end of your working day, when you are feeling tired, grumpy and generally "out of sorts" with yourself and other people, and when the very last thing you want to do is to exercise – that you *should* get yourself into that gym!

Why?

Because it is precisely at this time, when your brain and body are "down." and your oxygen supply is becoming like low-grade gas, that your entire blood/body/brain system needs a fresh supply of high-grade fuel – good oxygen, pumped into every muscle fiber and every brain cell!

Many people who overcome the "don't want to exercise" syndrome at the end of work find that they are reinvigorated after exercising, are far more relaxed and happy, and are delighted to be in the company of others.

Try it and see!

9. Change your Pace

While it is important to exercise regularly, it is also important for you to vary the pace of your life. An appropriate analogy from aerobic training springs to mind: the strongest hearts are those that can continue not only for a long distance, but can also, over that distance, change pace. This gives not only long-term stamina, but long-term *flexible* stamina.

Your brain requires similar changes of pace, and you can make it fitter both in terms of strength *and* flexibility. This does not mean letting your behavior become random, but rather allowing for those special activities that are not part of the regular routine.

10. Healthy Diet

A healthy, well-balanced diet is as vital to your Physical Intelligence as a healthy, fit, agile and co-ordinated body is. Dieticians and nutritionists are urging us all to eat much more oily fish, olive oil and fresh fruit and vegetables, to protect ourselves against heart disease and cancer. It is very noticeable that the Japanese, whose diet is rice and vegetable-based, have the best health records in the world – followed by people around the Mediterranean, who tend to eat far more fish and fresh vegetables than the rest of Western Europe and America.

To eat more healthily, cut down on red meat and fatty foods (like fries, hamburgers and cookies), and go for chicken or fish instead. Explore books, courses and the web for the latest information on what your body needs as food/fuel. Start from the basic idea that fresh foods are generally best, vegetables make the most appropriate foundation for your diet, and that variety is important. Exploring international cuisine will also, add spice to your life (literally in many cases).

11. Body Consciousness

This phrase can have both a positive and a negative meaning. Everything you have read so far in this chapter is pleading for you to be conscious of your body. If you are, and if you follow the path suggested, you will be both conscious and *proud* of your body.

The other meaning is of course of being *self*-conscious – being embarrassed because you feel overweight, flabby, unfit and unattractive. If you do feel like this, you will obviously not want to go anywhere near gyms, swimming pools or keep-fit classes. If you do feel self-conscious, start a very gentle exercise programme in the privacy of your own home: take a brisk walk for at least 15 minutes every day, or a mild jog; make sure you take the stairs rather than the elevator at work, etc. Combined with a healthier diet, this will make a big difference. Give yourself a positive goal, for example to increase your walking/jogging distance by a half, or to lose five pounds in weight.

Although such starting out exercise is certainly beneficial, it will not really increase your flexibility, or strength or your cardiovascular health. You will need to add some real physical health training to your weekly exercise schedule to do this. However, having achieved your first set of goals, you should be confident enough to go to a formal exercise class!

12. Fear of Strain/Damage

If you are worried that an exercise programme will damage your health, go to your doctor and make sure you get a good medical check-up and some thorough advice before starting. *Always*, even if you have been reasonably fit before, start gently. It is far better to ease into a gradual programme of becoming happily fit than to go at it like a bull in a china shop.

13. Training the Body to Want Physical Exercise

The good news here is that you don't have to! It has been shown that it takes just 21 days for something to become a habit, and when you find the right exercise/sport for you, you will find that you feel so invigorated, so much more alive and so much better in yourself, that you will become addicted to exercise!

During the first two to three weeks of your programme, make sure that your exercise date is in your diary, and that you give yourself those extra little nudges to help get you to the state where you'll be adding *extra* exercise sessions because you love it so much!

14. Relaxation and Stress Reduction

Stress is now well known to be a body and brain killer: make sure that it doesn't get you. You can do this by taking regular breaks during the day, by listening to relaxing music, by taking regular exercise, by reading novels, by taking walks in nature, by spending good social time with friends, and by laughing! Try them all!

If you can't take a break during the day because you are stuck at work, try a few simple exercises – tensing and relaxing your shoulders, arms and legs in turn, or deliberately breathing deeply in and out for 10 breaths – just to give yourself a mini "time-out." It is amazing how much benefit such quick and easy activities can bring.

15. The Rest/Activity Cycle

In planning your Physical Intelligence development programme, consider the balance between your rest periods and activity periods. In our work-oriented society we have tended to emphasize activity while disparaging rest. We like to "see the job through" and often consider breaks as a sign of laziness and sloth.

Mentally speaking, your brain can continue actively for between 20 and 60 minutes before it literally becomes drained of oxygen and physiological resources, *requiring* rest. As you will have realized from the previous comments on creativity and problem solving (*see Chapter 1*), and the difference between recall and understanding (*in Chapter 10*), your brain requires a proper rest/activity cycle in order to function at full force. Rest is *not* "doing nothing" – it is a process in which your brain recuperates, reorganizes, integrates, makes things complete, and prepares for the next left-brain activity cycle.

Breaks can be just a change of activity, which allows the side of your brain you have been using to rest, while you use the brain's other side. Or it can be a full break in which you let your entire brain idle. Those occasional (and preferably more regular) drifts into day-dreams are actually the brain protecting itself against undue wear and tear. You *need* those periods of day-dreaming. Often when you lose concentration, it is your brain telling you that it is time to take a break.

16. The Long-life Quiz

Some psychologists have come to the view that we all have the capacity to live to be 100. Biologists now set the upper limit for human life even higher – maybe as high as 125. Indeed, they are in excellent company. Although the biblically sanctioned life-span is normally said to be "three score years and ten" (i.e. 70), Genesis mentions that man's days "shall be an hundred and twenty years." After years of research on longevity I have drawn up the following quiz, based on questions asked by life-insurers to work out the chances of someone living for a set number of years. My own view is that people who are intellectually and physically active and contented have the best chance of living to be 100 or more.

Start by looking up your present age in the life-expectancy chart on the next page. Against this, you will find your basic life-expectancy, derived from figures produced by insurance actuaries. Then answer the questions on the following pages, and add to or take away from this basic figure, according to how your own lifestyle and personality affect your habits.

Remember: women can expect to live roughly three years longer than men (on whom the table is based). Women should therefore add three years to their basic life-expectancy figure.

Basic Life-expectancy Chart

Age (present)	Life expectancy (estimated)	Age (present)	Life expectancy (estimated)	Age (present)	Life expectancy (estimated)	Age (present)	Life expectancy (estimated)
15	70.7	35	72.1	55	74.9	75	82.8
16	70.8	36	72.2	56	75.1	76	83.3
17	70.8	37	72.2	57	75.4	77	83.9
18	70.8	38	72.3	58	75.5	78	84.5
19	70.9	39	72.4	59	76.0	79	85.1
20	71.1	40	72.5	60	76.3	80	85.7
21	71.1	41	72.6	61	76.6	81	86.3
22	71.2	42	72.7	62	77.0	82	87.0
23	71.3	43	72.8	63	77.3	83	87.6
24	71.3	44	72.9	64	77.7	84	88.2
25	71.4	45	73.0	65	78.1		
26	71.5	46	73.2	66	78.4		
27	71.6	47	73.3	67	78.9		
28	71.6	48	73.5	68	79.3		
29	71.7	49	73.6	69	79.7		
30	71.8	50	73.8	70	80.2		
31	71.8	51	74.0	71	80.7		
32	71.9	52	74.2	72	81.2		
33	72.0	53	74.4	73	81.7		
34	72.0	54	74.7	74	82.2		

How to Calculate Your Own Life Expectancy

1 Add one year for each of your grandparents who lived to be 80 or more, or is 80 and still alive. Add half a year for each one who topped 70, or is 70 and still alive.

2 Take off four years if any of your sisters, brothers, parents or grandparents died of a heart attack, stroke or arteriosclerosis before the age of 50.

Subtract two years for each of these relatives who died of these causes between the ages of 50 and 60.

3 Take off three years for each sister, brother, parent or grandparent who died of *diabetes mellitus* or a peptic ulcer before aged 60. If any of these died of stomach cancer before 60, subtract two years. For any other illnesses that killed them before 60 (except those caused by accidents) subtract one year.

4 Women who cannot have children, or who plan none, subtract half a year. Women with over seven children, take off one year.

5 If you are a first-born, add one year.

6 Add two years if your traditional intelligence is above average (i.e., if you have an IQ of over 100).

7 Smoking: take off 12 years (yes, *12*) if you smoke more than 40 cigarettes a day; if it is 20–40 cigarettes, subtract seven years; fewer than 20 per day, subtract two years.

8 If you enjoy regular sex once or twice a week, add two years.

9 If you have a thorough annual medical check-up, add two years.

10 If you are overweight, take off two years.

11 If you sleep more than 10 hours every night, or less than 5 hours a night, take off two years.

12 Drinking: one or two measures of spirits, or half a litre of wine, or up to a maximum of four glasses of beer per day, counts as moderate – add three years. If you don't drink every day – add only one and a half years. If you don't drink at all, don't add or subtract anything. Heavy drinkers and alcoholics – take off eight years.

13 Exercise: three times a week – jogging, cycling, swimming, brisk walks, dancing, skating, etc. – add three years. (Weekend walks don't count!)

14 Do you eat simple, plain foods, vegetables and fruit rather than richer, meatier, fatty foods? If you can say yes honestly, and stop eating before you are full, add one year.

15 If you are frequently ill (with more than the odd cold!), take off five years.

16 Education: if you did postgraduate work at university, add three years. For a first degree, add two. Up to A-level, add one. Below that neither add nor subtract anything.

17 Jobs: if you are a professional person, add one and a half years; technical, managerial, administrative and agricultural workers, add one year; proprietors, clerks and sales staff, add nothing; semi-skilled workers, take off half a year; manual workers, subtract four years. If you're not a manual worker but your job involves a lot of physical work, add two years. If it is a desk job, take off two years.

18 If you live in a town, or have done so for most of your life, take off one year. Add a year if most of your time has been spent in the countryside.

19 If you are married and living with your spouse, add one year. However, if you are a separated man living alone, take off nine years; seven if you are a widower living alone. If you live with others, take off only half of these figures. Women who are separated or divorced, take off four years; widows, three and a half, unless you live with others, in which case take off only two.

20 If you have one or two close friends in whom you confide, add a year.

21 Add two years if you keep your mind active, e.g., if you play chess or backgammon, or do crossword puzzles regularly.

22 If your attitude to life is both positive and realistic, add four years.

Armed with this information you can now calculate your own life expectancy. Remember to add on three years if you are a woman.

Note: The results of this quiz are a guide to your probable life expectancy *if you continue* your patterns of behavior as they are at present. Remember – nothing is unimprovable; even though longevity is usually regarded as genetic, it is often more the case of copying lifestyle patterns. So if your parents smoked, you are more likely to do so, or if your parents brought you up on a healthy diet full of vegetables and fresh fruit, you are more likely to still eat healthily.

Considering your Life-expectancy Questionnaire

If part of your goal is to live a happy, healthy and long life, then checking the Life-expectancy Questionnaire can provide useful information to guide your future behaviour.

The following are brief ideas on improving life expectancy by improving your mental and physical activity:

- Your intelligence can be improved by using your left and right brains together, and by increasing your vocabulary. Expand your education too – it is never too late to learn something new, and it will keep your mind fit and active.
- If you smoke, both your physical and mental health can be improved by stopping.
- Yes, make sure that you include time for lovemaking. Because this seems so obvious, many tend to take it as a given, and in assuming this, they neglect it.
- Plan for a regular medical check-up, maintain a reasonable weight, and make sure you get a reasonable amount of sleep each night.
- Exercise is exceptionally important and should be a major part of your self-development programme.
- A simple, relatively plain, vegetable- and fruit-dominated diet will keep you both mentally and physically alert.
- Make sure that your job includes a reasonable balance of mental and physical activity; make sure you spend time in the country (it's good for the right brain as well as the lungs!)
- If you do not have close friends, improving your Social Intelligence (as explained in Chapter 3) will help you expand the number and "quality" of your friends.
- Once again, make sure you get regular rests and are able to enjoy yourself when you take it easy.

On to your Physical Intelligence Questionnaire. Remember that a score of 50 per cent or more means that you are doing truly well. A score of 100 per cent means that you are a genius in this intelligence. Check yourself over time, and enter your scores on the table on page **221**.

MULTIPLE INTELLIGENCE TEST - PHYSICAL INTELLIGENCE

Score yourself between 0–100; 0 would mean that the statement was absolutely untrue and did not apply to you at all, and 100 would mean that you agreed with the statement completely and utterly.

I exercise aerobically (cardiovascularly) at least four times a week for 30 minutes or more, at a hard and fast pace.   SCORE ......

I am physically co-ordinated, balanced and poised.   SCORE ......

I am exceptionally strong at lifting, pulling and pushing with every one of my major bodily muscle groups.   SCORE ......

I am unusually flexible in all joints.   SCORE ......

My resistance to major and minor illnesses means that I am consistently in excellent health, and rarely miss a day off work sick.   SCORE ......

My stamina is extraordinary. I can go on and on in physical, mental, sexual, social and professional situations.   SCORE ......

My diet is particularly well-balanced, varied and healthy, and would be the envy of an Olympic athlete. It incorporates fresh food, little sugar and salt and few refined foods.   SCORE ......

I manage my activity/rest time intelligently, incorporating regular and good sleep, at least three good breaks during a working day, and at least four weeks a year in which I am completely away from my main profession or pastime.   SCORE ......

I relish all thoughts of physical activity and consider the
expression of myself in physical/sporting/dancing activity
to be a major theme of my life.   SCORE ......

I manage my energy well, so that, like a cat, I am always willing
and able to leap into action at any time.   SCORE ......

TOTAL SCORE ......

making sense
of your senses

your sensual intelligence

SENSUAL INTELLIGENCE - A DEFINITION

Leonardo da Vinci noted, with some melancholy, that the average human "looks without seeing, listens without hearing, touches without feeling, eats without tasting, moves without physical awareness, inhales without awareness of odor or fragrance and talks without thinking."

Is this you?!

Your Sensory Intelligence concerns your ability to use each of your five physical senses (and your "sixth sense" – intuition) to the full extent of their quite incredible powers.

WHAT'S IN IT FOR YOU?

This chapter will introduce you to some amazing facts about your senses and how to develop them for your benefit and, equally importantly, for your pleasure. Your senses may well be millions of times more "intelligent" than you had ever thought, and you will leave your Brain Workout having learned how to feast your senses and to make your life a treat for your body.

A SENSORY INTELLIGENCE STAR

Many people think of Walt Disney as a city-born businessman and movie producer, with a creative flair for entertaining children and their families. This is partly true, but the whole truth is much more interesting, and reveals a genius of Sensual Intelligence.

Walt Disney was actually born, and spent most of his childhood, on a farm in Missouri. As soon as he had finished school, he went not into business or to university, but to an art school, where he immersed himself in the exploration of visual and tactile media.

Walt rapidly realized that his talents lay in translating the senses into film. He was the first to introduce sound into cartoons, when he featured Mickey Mouse in *Steamboat Willy*. Again he scored a visual first when he filmed *Flowers and Trees* (1932): this was the first movie of *any* kind to be made in complete Technicolor®.

He continued his sensually pioneering ways, producing in 1940 *Fantasia*, a movie generally thought to be nearly half-a-century ahead of its time! In *Fantasia* Disney created a feast for the senses, asking the viewer to imagine what anyone might imagine while listening to beautiful music. Using cartoon technology that to this day has not been matched, he accomplished the brilliant feat of transforming one sense into another. He was able with his cartoon techniques to make the viewer *see* sound, *taste* vision, *hear* shapes, *feel* color, and *touch* rhythm.

Continuing his mission to use and stimulate all the senses in and by his work, after the war Disney began to use a series of short real-life movies that showed hitherto unseen close-ups of animals in natural settings. In order to bring the senses more realistically to life, he insisted that his artists observe every vision, movement and sound of the animals so as to absorb their most subtle and *real* nuances. Those who worked with him were in awe of his Multiple Intelligences. They reported that Disney kept entire multi-sensory movies, second-by-second, detail-by-detail, sense-by-sense, perfectly in his memory.

THE MAGIC OF YOUR SENSES

You are a walking miracle! If you in any way doubt this, read the following information about your senses and change your mind. You are *far* smarter than you think!

Your Eyes

This is what Leonardo da Vinci, probably the greatest Brain of All Time, said about this one aspect of you:

Do you not see that the eye encompasses the beauty of the whole world: it is the master of astronomy, it assists and directs all the arts of man. It sends men forth to all the corners of the earth. It reigns over the various departments of mathematics, and all its sciences are the most infallible. It has measured the distance of the size of the stars; has discovered the elements and the nature thereof; and from the courses of the constellations it has enabled us to predict things to come. It has created architecture and perspective, and lastly, the divine art of painting. O, thou most excellent of all God's creations! What hymns can do justice to thy nobility; what peoples, what tongues, sufficiently describe thine achievements?

When you read the following facts about your eyes, think about whether any camera or computer can even *nearly* begin to match them for complexity and sophistication. Also try to estimate how much it would cost, using all the latest scientific equipment, to produce a piece of equipment that could duplicate their function.

- Your retina, the light-receiving surface at the back of your eye, is only slightly thicker than a razor blade, yet contains **130,000,000** photo-receptor (light receiving) cells.
- Of these 130,000,000 cells, a mere **6,000 000** of them, called the cones, handle *all* color vision.
- These 6,000,000 cones can process and distinguish **8,000,000** different shades of color.
- The remaining 124,000,000 photoreceptors are called rods. They are so sensitive that they can detect and distinguish a *single* photon of light.
- At night the 124,000,000 rods, in order to help you survive in the dark, can increase their sensitivity **75,000** times.
- Every *second* billions of photons of light strike your retina. This is the equivalent of about **100 megabytes** of information per second!

To make all this amazing information even more amazing, it isn't actually your eyes that "see" – it is your brain. Your eye sends all its multiple gigabytes of information along your optic nerve to the back of your brain, where what is called your occipital lobe actually does your seeing for you. This it does with a few billion brain cells that perfectly reproduce reality for you.

DID YOU KNOW?

A scientist at the Cern Laboratory recently estimated that to duplicate all the functions of the human eye using the latest laser, fiber optic and computer technology would involve a piece of equipment the size of a normal room, and costing over $73,000,000! This was probably an underestimate.

If ever anybody dares to call you worthless, you can simply point to one eye and say "I'm sorry. $73,000,000 right *there*!"

Your Ears

The *Sunday Times* newspaper recently said of your ear, *"structurally, the human sound system seems like the result of a back-of-an-envelope sketch by a genius inventor. A collecting device, a tunnel, a membrane, three bones, a window, some fluid, a spiral tube with more membrane, rows of hairs and finally pathways to the brain."*

Another way of looking at it is as a marvel of miniaturization. Compressed into two cubic centimeters you have a wide-range sound-wave analyzer, a noise-reduction system, two-way communication, a relay unit, a multi-channel transducer and a hydraulic balance system!

- You have **16,000** hair cells in your inner ear – they respond faster than any other cell in your body.
- Any of the 16,000 hair cells will trigger if you move the tip by as little as the *width* of an atom! That's the equivalent of being able to detect the movement at the top of the world's tallest skyscraper if it moved less than one and a half centimeters.
- Your hair cells, when you listen to the high notes in classical music, fire at the rate of **20,000 times a second.**
- Your ear receives information in one dimension, and yet you hear 3-D sound and can instantaneously locate its origin. How? Because your amazing ear–brain system can distinguish the different time by which the "same" sound arrived in each ear. The difference that you can distinguish is **200-millionths** of a second!

Your Nose

- Your nose has **5,000,000** olfactory receptors: each one has its own gene.
- Over **1,000** giant protein molecules are used by your receptors to decode smell.
- Your nose can distinguish **10,000** different odors.

- In ways that no scientist has yet been able to explain, your nose can detect one molecule of "smell" in one part per *trillion* of air!
- Your olfactory nerves are unique. One end of each of them is exposed to the outside world. The other speeds the impulses directly into your brain, providing an instantaneous communications link between the two. The things you smell can bring about deep and powerful emotional responses. This is because the minute your brain is aware of a smell, it sends the information directly to your emotional center. This is in part why aromas are so closely associated with sexual arousal and the powers of recall.

Your Mouth

Your brain considers your mouth to be the second most important part of your body – second only to your hands. The mouth combines the early warning and defense systems of the lips, teeth, gums and tongue.

- Your mouth contains up to **10,000** super-sensitive taste buds.
- These 10,000 taste buds can detect:

  sweet flavours at one part per 200

  salt at one part per 400

  sour at one part per 130,000

  bitter at one part per 2,000,000.
- The taste buds combine with your olfactory system to allow you to distinguish **millions** of different taste sensations.

To show you the extraordinary sensitivity of your mouth, let me tell you about some intriguing research.

The Tea Story

In England, people are often concerned whether it is "proper" or "better" to pour the milk or the tea in first to a cup. Some time ago a group of tea drinkers got into a major argument about it; those who said that the milk should be put in first insisted that they could *always* tell the difference. It was decided to put them to the test.

To everybody's amazement, the tea drinkers were nearly 100 per cent accurate in identifying which liquid had been put in first. In order to find out exactly how they did this, researchers decided to find out exactly what happens when either milk or tea is poured first. They filmed the process of pouring milk into tea and tea into milk, and then played it back in slow motion.

They observed that no matter how fast the liquid was poured in, a few drops always raced to the head of the tea-fall or the milk-fall, and entered the other liquid first. When the first few drops of milk entered the boiling cup of tea, they were immediately burnt before the remaining volume of the milk could plunge in and cool the liquid down. These tiny drops gave a very delicate burnt/singed milk tinge to the taste of the tea. In contrast, when the tiny boiling drops of tea hit the giant cool lake of milk, they were immediately cooled and none of the milk was burnt.

The tea tasters were right – the incredible human body and its senses triumphed once again!

Your Skin

Your skin is the largest organ of your body.

- It contains **200,000** temperature receivers.
- It contains **500,000** touch and pressure receivers.
- It contains **2,800,000** pain receivers.
- This total of **3,500,000** receivers over the surface of your body is in addition to the multiple millions of receivers for your eyes, ears, nose and mouth.

Touch is directly connected to your emotions. Touch is also a life-giving ability. Young animals and human babies who receive little physical affection in the form of touch in their early lives become unhealthy and fail to thrive. (How do *you* feel when you are touched by someone you love? Or when you are *not* touched by anyone, in any way, for days on end?)

case study

The Italian designer Giorgio Armani is renowned for the outstanding, sensual nature of his clothes. The soft, tactile materials he uses are immensely appealing to the senses of sight and touch. He selects materials that also are appealing to the sense of smell, and supplements these with a range of enticing perfumes.

Your Intuition

Your sixth sense – your intuition – which is so often incorrectly equated with emotion, is in fact based on logic, and not only logic, but Super Logic!

Research has shown that the upper part of your brain, the cerebral cortex, is divided into two distinct paths, joined by a sophisticated network of nerves that shuttles information between the two sides. This giant "thinking cap" is the most developed part of your brain and contains your full range of mental skills, such as logic and analysis. These intellectual skills are supplemented by your five senses to create your intuition. Working together they help you to survive in the world around you.

So what actually happens in an intuitive situation? Imagine, for example, entering a room where you suddenly "feel" that it is either welcoming or somehow threatening. In such a situation, your brain completes the most amazing calculation.

In a split second, using all your cortical skills and senses, plus the database of your entire life-to-date, it performs an instant compare/contrast with the many new items the room presents to you. (Pure, magnificent, Numerical Intelligence!) Your brain then produces a probability estimate of your chances of survival in that room. Depending on the "probability print-out" you will either relax, or have the hair stand up on the back of your neck.

Research has shown that acting upon what is mistakenly called "Gut Feeling" (from now on you can call it "Brain Feeling") is the correct decision more than 80 per cent of the time, and that if you train your intuition, this success rate rises.

Now that you realize what a billion-faceted and almost impossibly magnificent piece of equipment your body, your senses and you are, it is time to put them all to use in the manner for which they were designed. It is time for the Brain and Sense Workout.

BRAIN AND SENSE WORKOUT – EXPANDING YOUR SENSORY INTELLIGENCE

1. Explore and Develop all your Senses

Explore and develop the capacities and sensitivities of all your senses. Use the Senses Grid illustrated below in all the environments in which you spend considerable amounts of time. These will probably include the various rooms of your home; your place of work; your places of entertainment; and those places to which you go on vacation.

In each of your environments ask yourself the following. Does this room/place/environment fully stimulate and satisfy the intelligences of my:

- eyes   yes/no
- ears   yes/no
- nose   yes/no
- mouth   yes/no
- skin   yes/no
- intuition   yes/no

"Rooms":	Office	Living room	Kitchen	Bedroom	Bathroom	Yard	Den	Dining room	Mobile home	Car	Boat	Restaurant
Senses:												
Eyes												
Ears												
Nose												
Mouth												
Skin												
Intuition												

Armed with your answers, decide whether or not you wish to change any of these major areas in your life. Where appropriate, apply the Senses Grid to the environments of your loved ones and children. The Sensual Home Mind Map® (color plate 6) will give you some ideas to think about – and maybe to try out at home.

2. Give your Eyes Regular Visual Feasts

- Practice distinguishing colors.
- Take an introductory art course.
- Use colorful words in your conversation – this will keep your eyes alert.
- Make your food, as well as tasteful, *colorful*. A meal containing different colored foods has been shown to be more likely to contain all the different minerals, vitamins and nutrients our bodies need than monochrome meals. Hospitals take note: serving bland food makes the body bland!
- Try the following da Vinci vision training exercise.

To sharpen his eyes and focus, Leonardo placed a complex object, like a bowl of flowers, in front of him, tried to memorize it, and then closed his eyes. With his eyes closed he tried to revisualize the object. Leonardo would then open his eyes and compare the memory with the real vision. He then looked even more closely, correcting the memory, and once again closed his eyes and revisualized the scene. He kept on doing this until he could hardly tell the difference between the vision he saw with his open eyes and the vision he saw with his mind's memory.

Try it! It sharpens both your external *and* internal vision. You can try similar exercises with your hearing and taste.

3. Give your Ears Regular Aural Treats

Try the following:

- Learn to discriminate the different sounds in nature, especially bird song.
- Listen to more ethnic and classical music – widen your aural horizons.
- Listen to excellent recordings on the best equipment, and attend live concerts. This will keep those tens of thousands of sound receptors happily fit and energized, firing away at their 20,000 times a second.
- Take care of your ears and hearing by making sure that you do not listen to music that is too loud for too long. If you are in a disco or a band where this is the case, use some earplugs.

- Occasionally give your ears the treat of *no sound* – like the rest of your body they need rest, and will reward you well for providing them with it!

- Doctors and health workers are increasingly of the opinion that certain sounds can have a very positive effect on your health. Dentists have found that playing soothing music during appointments helps to relax patients, and Russian scientists have even experimented by playing the "sound" of a healthy muscle in action to a corresponding damaged muscle, to help it heal. They found that these damaged muscles healed more quickly than muscles which did not have the sounds played to them!

4. Provide your Nose with Olfactory Surprises

- Regularly give your nose (as well as the rest of you!) the treat of trips into nature. Inhale through your nose as all animals do, rather than through your mouth, as most people do. Sniff the rain. You think it doesn't have its own aroma? Yes it does!

- Learn to distinguish the smells of different essential oils. Try using them.

- Learn to distinguish the scents of different flowers.

- Smell has become one of the least used senses. Reverse this trend! Experiment by placing flowers around your home, and by using perfumed candles in chosen rooms or when you are having a bath. If you have a garden, plant it to create scent treats – see the Planning a Garden Mind Map®, color plate 10.

- Become more sensitive to the smells that turn you off and smells that turn you on. Work out whether this is because of the smell itself, or because of some positive or negative association you have with that smell. In all your "olfactory environments" do your best to accentuate the positive!

5. Provide Regular Treats for your Mouth

- Experiment with dishes from as many different nations as you can. Not only will this widen the "intelligence" of your palette, it will simultaneously increase the intelligence of your olfactory system.

- Regularly prepare foods with many different textures.
- Care for your mouth, tongue and gums with regular check-ups and daily brushing and flossing, done correctly.
- Where appropriate, eat food with your hands. Your hands are an advanced monitoring system for your stomach, and their millions of touch receptors will alert your entire digestive system to the forthcoming pleasures. Eating with your hands will also provide the essential natural oils for the skin of your hands, lips and face.
- If you drink alcohol, develop your wine-tasting skills. This can be beautifully linked to your Creative and Verbal Intelligences.

Wine tasters tend to use common words and phrases to describe the different tastes of wines, such as "sweet," "dry," "heavy," "lemony," "nutty," "sharp," "sticky," "fruity," etc. Rather than falling into this norm-al descriptive trap, try to find new and imaginative ways of explaining what your mouth *really* feels. See if you can beat some of the best ones I have heard, like:

"This wine tastes as clean as a bird's song sounds."

"This wine is so full bodied that it feels as if it should be eaten rather than drunk!"

Or even, "This wine grabs the back of my throat like a ferret grabbing its prey."

Of course, you don't have to limit yourself to describing wines – try anything else that you can think of: cheeses, breads, beers, chocolates, whatever.

6. Give your Skin Regular Treats

Experiment with the following:

- Make sure that your clothes are of varying, stimulating and comfortable textures so that you are giving a constant treat to your 3,500,000 touch receivers.

- Try wearing "breathable" natural fabrics like cotton, in order to give your skin freedom and the chance to breathe.
- Regularly give your skin and hair a feast of oils – they will reward you for the thrill.

7. Develop your Intuition

- Stand with your eyes shut, and ask a friend, starting some feet away, to approach slowly and silently. You then say "stop" when you feel that they are only an arm's length away. You'll be amazed at how rapidly your brain can learn to do this.
- Become more aware of listening to and acting on your intuition.
- Each time your intuition is correct, try to analyze what it was that made you accurate, and add it to your "intuition database."

8. Heighten All your Sense Receptors

- Test yourself on distinguishing different smells. For example, look at a vase of flowers and try to associate what you see with what you smell. Close your eyes and, by smelling the aroma of the flowers, try to remember what you have seen – thus enhancing the link between your sense of smell and your intuition. Then open your eyes to see how accurate you were. Continue this process until you can hardly tell the difference between when your eyes are open and when they are closed. Do similar exercises with your other senses.
- Choose vacation locations and activities that stimulate your entire range of senses.

Developing your senses in the ways outlined has another remarkable benefit – it gives you a Masterful Memory! If you think about it, you will realize that your memories are triggered by your senses. A tune plays and you remember that afternoon by the river; a smell wafts toward you and suddenly you recall an entire episode of your school life; you see a picture and your brain is flooded with memories; you taste a particular dish and suddenly you are a time-traveller, transported back into your own history.

As you develop your Sensory Intelligence, you will be effortlessly growing and empowering the muscles of your Memory and Mind.

Next follows your Sensual Intelligence Questionnaire. Remember that a score of 50 per cent or more means that you are doing truly well. A score of 100 per cent means that you are a genius in this intelligence. Check yourself over time to watch your scores rise and enter them on the table on page **221.**

MULTIPLE INTELLIGENCE TEST – SENSUAL INTELLIGENCE

Fill in the following questionnaire. If the statement for you is explosively true, give yourself a score of 100; if the statement is absolutely and incontrovertibly untrue for you, give yourself a score of 0.

I enjoy dancing, with a passion.   SCORE ......

I would describe myself as "sartorially intelligent" – a genius at clothes selection and even design. My clothes are color co-ordinated, tactile, and regularly receive positive comments from those around me.

SCORE ......

I blend the senses to improve the richness of my life and my memory.   SCORE ......

I see/hear/smell/feel/taste things that many would not consider having these attributes. For example I might associate emotions and colors with numbers and sounds.   SCORE ......

I am able to recall visual information with immediacy and stunning clarity.   SCORE ......

I can identify subtle differences in tastes and am sensitive to food combinations.   SCORE ......

I am especially sensitive to smells, and the olfactory sense plays a large role in my major life memories.   SCORE ......

As I create my own environment and living style, I constantly consider the textures and colors of clothes, decorations and food. SCORE ......

I am particularly aware of sounds and music, and of their ability to influence and change my moods and environment. I use this knowledge to help improve my life and to make it more varied. SCORE ......

I would be placed in the top percentile of those who live to eat; the bottom percentile of those who eat only to live. SCORE ......

I consider myself a particularly sensual person; touching and being touched is a part of my way of communicating with others. SCORE ......

I love all aspects of nature and am regularly in contact with the land, rivers, lakes and the oceans. I also like all forms of weather. SCORE ......

I regularly describe experiences in one sense with the language of another. SCORE ......

I am very intuitive and have strong gut-level responses to things. I often sense what the correct line of action is, and will in general tend to follow that line, even if logic apparently dictates against it. SCORE ......

TOTAL SCORE ......

your sexual intelligence

SEXUAL INTELLIGENCE - A DEFINITION

What is it that:

- makes you live longer?
- has inspired many of the greatest works of art, music and literature?
- makes your skin glow?
- has inspired renaissances and revolutions?
- improves body tone?
- sells more products than anything else?
- promotes cardiovascular conditioning?
- reduces stress?
- is thought about by most people dozens of times a day?
- still remains a mystery?
- and is the main reason the human race still exists?

You got it – SEX!

As you can see from the list above, your Sexual Intelligence is a "Super Intelligence." It is a combination and a manifestation of *all* your other Intelligences. It is not, as has been commonly supposed, a genital-led lust; it is a great driving energy which marshals all your intellectual and physical resources to ensure your survival, your family's survival, and the survival of the human race.

The biggest sexual organ on the planet is not between your legs – it's between your ears!

WHAT'S IN IT FOR YOU?

This chapter explores what many consider to be the prime (if not primal!) intelligence. We will disclose some fascinating discoveries about sex and age, and in the Sexual Brain Workout you learn how to use each of your other multiple intelligences to improve your Sexual Intelligence and performance.

Let's take a look at a wonderful example of someone with a great Sexual Intelligence.

A SEXUAL INTELLIGENCE STAR

Marilyn Monroe is regarded by many as the great sexual icon of the 20th century. Is this simply because of her body and her "vital statistics?"

There were and are many actresses with equal or even "better" bodies, so it was obviously not just Marilyn's body that was a factor. What distinguished Marilyn Monroe from the others was the way in which she *used her multiple intelligences* to make herself sexually irresistible.

Marilyn was exceptionally creative, and used her skills as a comedienne and sense of comic timing to bring a wonderful light touch to her film roles. Socially

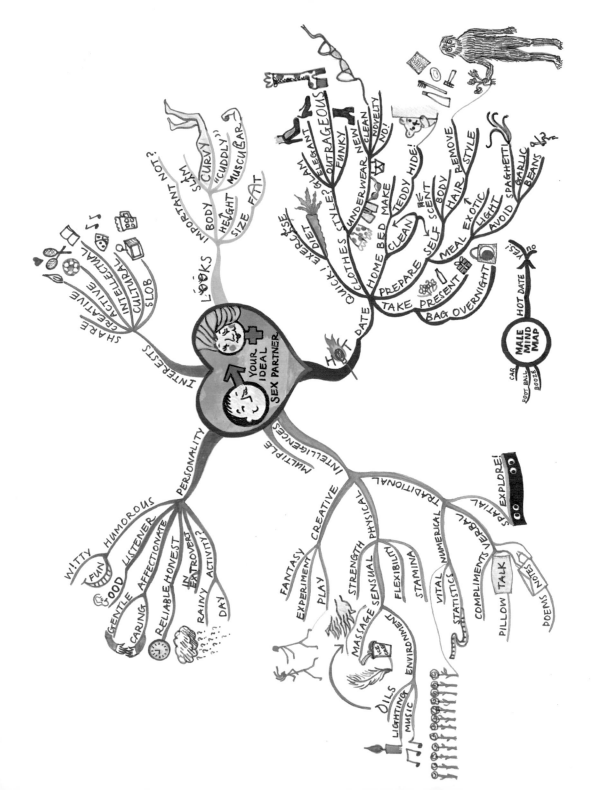

Plate 7

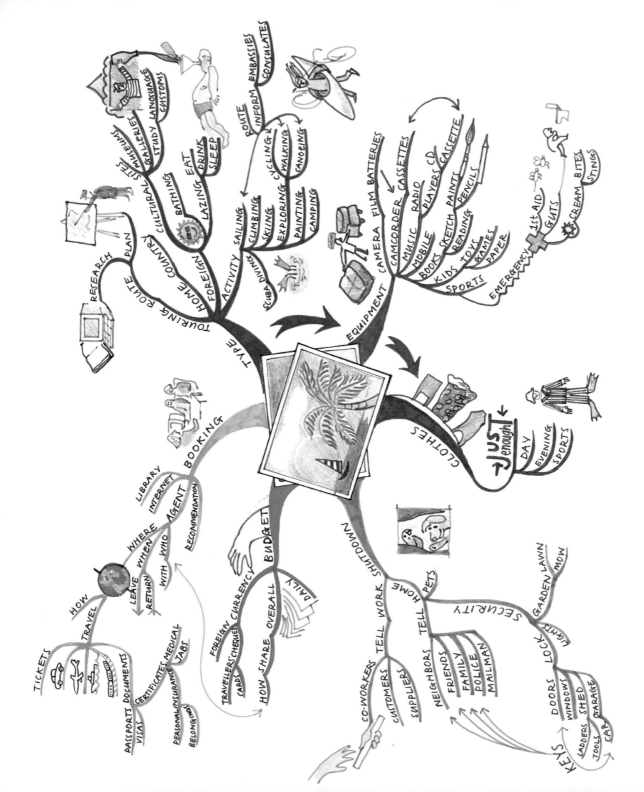

Plate 8

Marilyn was extremely adept, and was known as the life and soul of the many parties she attended. This was largely due to her skill at understanding other people, and her exceptional wit and playfulness.

What many people do not know is that Marilyn was a master of physical control, especially control of the facial muscles. Those who study the science of human expression reveal that there are millions of muscle fibers in the human face, and that they can all be controlled. Marilyn practiced this art to an extraordinary degree. She could create, at will, any "come hither" facial gesture that she felt like. As millions of fans will testify, it worked!

In addition to being extremely Physically Intelligent, Marilyn Monroe was also a great user of her Sensual Intelligence. In her films she used her voice like a musical instrument, arranged sensual scenes in which the senses of sight, taste, smell and touch were provocatively aroused, and she delighted in letting the imagination run wild!

It is mistakenly assumed that her "traditional IQ" was low, and that she was a "dumb blonde." Nothing could be farther from the truth! Marilyn Monroe had an IQ at Mensa (the high IQ society) genius level, and used it to make those people less intelligent than herself *feel* that they were actually more intelligent than she was.

The great tragedy of Marilyn Monroe is that her Personal Intelligence and Spiritual Intelligence were not as highly developed as the other intelligences, and it was this that eventually led to her early death.

JUST WHAT *IS* SEXY?

This question was asked by international journalist Nanci Hellmich, who recently surveyed best-selling romantic fiction writers to discuss the qualities that were most sexually appealing in heroes and heroines. By now you can probably predict the answers!

The ideal hero is a strong, witty, intelligent character, with a good sense of humor who can communicate easily with other people. The ideal heroine was also seen as someone intelligent and fun, with a mind of her own.

It shouldn't come as much of a surprise by now that the characteristic people regard as most sexy is personality: it is not genitals and thighs but the brain and intelligence that come top of the sexual hit parade! And "Brain and Intelligence," as you now know, means Multiple Intelligences.

Why should this be?

Because for the survival of the human race (and that is what sex is really all about) each partner must select a lover whose chance of survival, on all levels, is good.

In order to be sexually attractive, therefore, all you need to do is what *Head First* has been suggesting all along – develop your multi-faceted Brain Power!

case study

Casanova is reported to be the most Sexually Intelligent person who ever lived. He made the in-depth study of the art and science of sexual seduction his life's mission, and as a result has a major place in human history. Casanova realized, before our modern knowledge of sex, that the art of seduction required the application of *all* the intelligences. He studied the role of the senses in "opening up" the minds and bodies of his intended lovers; he constantly devised creative new ways of lovemaking; he studied the art of words, conversation and logic, persuading women that not only must they, but that they *should* make love to him. When necessary he even brought spirituality into play, convincing his would-be lovers that if they made love to him God would be pleased! He is reputed to have been successful *thousands* of times.

In the Brain Workout next, we will look at each intelligence that we have already explored, and apply it to helping you become a charming, confident and irresistibly attractive lover.

THE BRAIN WORKOUT – DEVELOPING YOUR SEXUAL INTELLIGENCE

1. Creative Intelligence and Sex

- Fantasize!

You should now realize, from your work on your Creative Intelligence in Chapter 1, that your imagination is infinite. The good news for you here is that this means your brain's "library" of sexual "videos" is *also* infinite! So, don't get stuck in one "section" of your library. Let your imagination (which is your most powerful sexual ally), run riot! Doing so will release your inhibitions, and will allow you to "practice" variations on a sexual theme, which you can eventually share with your partner.

Sexual fantasizing, for many centuries a taboo subject, is now recognized by sexologists to be an extremely healthy activity that increases creativity both in the sexual arena and on a wider scale. Releasing your imagination is a wonderful way to start breaking free of the inhibitions and repressions that may have hindered your sex life in the past.

- Experiment!

Use your creative imagination to the full. Think of new positions and try them. Add variety to your love-life by making love in as many different creative locations as you can. The growing number of members in the "Mile High Club" (an informal group of people who have had sex in aeroplanes a mile or so above the earth's surface) attests to the brain's delight in sexual innovation!

- **Act out your fantasies!**

An ideal sexual partner is one who, like you, is opening his or her mind to the universe of sexual possibilities. With such a partner, explore sexual fantasies that are *mutually* appealing, and indulge yourselves!

- **Play!**

Boredom is the death of passion, but play is the death of boredom! Having fun and playing games is a wonderful way to add zest to your sexual life, and to increase the enjoyment of both yourself, your partner, and each of the other. Play is also another wonderful way of getting rid of repressions and inhibitions. Another advantage of play is that it relaxes you on a deep level, and relaxation leads to better sex.

Once again, use your creative imagination to generate as many different games as you can. As a starting point, maybe consider hide-and-seek/chase-me games. These alert the entire body and brain, both necessary preparations for good sex, and add the thrill of the hunt.

Role-playing is another good one. Many couples find playing roles such as doctor/nurse, teacher/pupil, dominator/dominated, hero/heroine, etc. highly stimulating. Imagine multiple possible roles, discuss them with your partner, select your favorites, and, as Shakespeare said: "*Let the play begin!*"

2. Personal Intelligence and Sex

Many societies have classified self-love, especially in the sexual sense, to be, like fantasizing, a sin. It is not! As Woody Allen once said: "*Don't mock masturbation: it's sex with someone I love!*"

Sexual self-love takes the form of both self-appreciation and self-stimulation. Studies have regularly shown that more than 90 per cent (and probably nearer 100 per cent!) of both men and women masturbate in some way. This can range from the simple form of gentle self-caressing, through to highly complex and sophisticated self-loving games and creative environments that lead to orgasm.

Sexual self-loving is a completely natural activity, and should be approached with the same creative energy as sex with a partner.

An additional advantage of sexual self-love is the discovery of things or situations that arouse you, which can then be transferred to form part of the sexual relationship with your partner.

3. Social Intelligence and Sex

Which person would you find more attractive as a fantasy or real sexual partner: one who never listened to you; who always manipulated situations so that he or she won and you lost; was uninterested in other people and was unable to express emotion and affection, *or* someone who listened sympathetically to you and your thoughts, concerns and feelings; was warm and open to all sorts of people; was full of personal warmth, charm and capacity for affection; and who put others at their ease in social gatherings?

Need I go on?!!

All surveys have shown that one of the most important sexual attractor is Social Intelligence. Indeed this particular intelligence is often equated with power, and power is, of course, one of the world's most potent aphrodisiacs.

As you develop your Social Intelligence, you will be creating around you a force field that will act like a giant magnet, drawing to you a widening range of possible sexual partners. You will increasingly generate an aura of confidence and openness. Enjoy the rewards!

4. Spiritual Intelligence and Sex

The world's great spiritual leaders have consistently proclaimed that there is one giant, fundamental principle to all spirituality: love.

A Spiritually Intelligent individual is one who is open to all things, is playful and humorous, deeply self-confident, and is constantly in awe of the magic of everything around them. Imagine such a lover, and you will immediately realize the sexual drawing-power of this intelligence.

Couples who have experienced both great Lust and great Love report that while sex without love can be a fantastic experience, lust *with* love adds a massive new dimension to the experience, embracing the ecstasy of the moment with an ongoing feeling of at-oneness with the universe. They report that their climax is magnified a million-fold, and continues as a "steady state" of ecstasy that pervades their lives.

Physiological studies have also shown that when you love, every molecule of your being opens up, so that every sense is more attuned and every brain cell more alert. Sex in this state will obviously be more complete and satisfying.

We are increasingly led to the conclusion, in complete contrast to that drawn for the past few centuries, that true spirituality, rather than being a rigid, frigid and non-sexual state, is a state of heightened sexuality and more responsive and responsible sexual activity.

5. Physical Intelligence and Sex

To emphasize the importance of Physical Intelligence in the sexual world, try to imagine a similar scenario to the one in the Social Intelligence section above.

Would you rather have a lover who was out of breath after a few minutes of passion, was physically uncoordinated and off balance, was consistently ill, and whose muscles were flabby and out of shape, *or* one who was fit and could continue with passionate lovemaking for as long as you desired, was physically co-ordinated, balanced and poised, was strong and confident, robustly healthy and seldom ill, and who loved all forms of physical activity?

Again the choice is obvious, and is confirmed by numerous surveys.

These "Analyses of Attraction" confirm that the fit, healthy body is a turn-on to both sexes. Interestingly, it is not any one particular factor but a combination of strength, flexibility, stamina, poise and general health that acts as a major sexual stimulant.

When we go back again to the main purpose of sex – the ongoing survival of the human race, it becomes immediately apparent why your prospective partners will be instinctively more turned on to you when you are energetically healthy. Other advantages of being physically fit are that it reduces stress levels, increases deep relaxation, increases blood supply to *all* your body parts and increases self-confidence. All of these help reduce inhibition, eliminate fear and increase sexual attraction and performance.

It really does come down to Survival of the Fittest!

DID YOU KNOW?

You were created when one of over 400 million sperms won the race to reach your mother's egg. You started out life already as a phenomenal winner!

6. Sensual Intelligence and Sex

The senses are your portals to sexual ecstasy. Use, stimulate and excite each one.

- **Your Eyes**

Your eyes are both a sexual stimulant to your partner and a great source of sexual pleasure. It is not the size of your eyes that attracts people; it is how big your pupils are. Your pupils enlarge when you are interested, and open fully when you are in love. Why? Because your brain, being totally absorbed, opens this "window of the mind" to let in more information.

The attraction of the dilated pupil explains why romantic candlelit dinners lead more easily to sex – the subdued light makes your pupils dilate, and you more seductive.

Visual stimulation is extremely important to both male and female sexual arousal. Sexually provocative clothes that hint at the body beneath; revealed flesh; sensuous movements; provocative eye and body language; and highlighted erotic areas (especially the lips, breasts and genitals), are all visual stimulants. General sexual imagery, in the form of erotic videos and pornographic magazines, will also stimulate your eyes.

- Sound

Sound is often rather forgotten as an aphrodisiac. However, good lovers use sound to their advantage. Many lovers use music to create a variety of moods. If you haven't already, try it!

Think how often great romantic scenes take place outdoors in a natural setting, with bees murmuring, brooks babbling, birds singing, and the lovers' hands and bodies counterpointing this music with the music of love. Mother Nature loves you to make love, and provides the music to accompany you.

- Smell

Your five million olfactory receptors are sexy little beings!

They are actually designed to "sniff out" healthy and sexy partners for you. You and your partner give off sexually arousing aromas called pheromones, which are like billions of Greek sirens beckoning you to the paradise of sexual gratification! Pheromones themselves are more "sexy" if your body is healthy and clean. They can be activated and enhanced by the use of natural oils (many of which have reported aphrodisiac qualities), including such fragrances as sandalwood, jasmine, neroli, musk and rose oils.

One recommended way of stimulating your sense of smell, especially before sex, is to have an oil-scented, warm bath before retiring.

- Mouth/skin/touch

Remember that your mouth and skin contain over three-and-a-half *million* sense receivers, each one waiting to serve you and your partner in your pursuit of sexual ecstasy!

Of the large amount of your brain devoted to looking after your body, more than half of it is devoted to your mouth and skin. Touch is brainy stuff!

Kissing. Your mouth is *by far* the most sensitive and versatile part of your body, and should be used as creatively and imaginatively as you can. Consider kissing to be not simply the clunking of one mouth on to another, but a major art, involving an infinite number of varied caresses, and an almost infinite number of "moods." Your kisses can be light, soft, tender, lingering, deep, "burning," passionate, smooth, rough, whatever.

Your lips and tongue can be used to stimulate not only the mouth but any area of your lover's body. Most men and women love kissing and love the full variety of kisses, and most lovers find that prolonged kissing can be extremely arousing, particularly a slow and intent movement from mouth kissing to overall body kissing, covering the entire skin, and inexorably heading, via the nipples and abdomen, feet, legs and inner thighs, to the genital area. If you are comfortable with oral sex, your mouth can provide your partner with one of the most intimate sexual experiences there is.

Massage. Massage is one of the ultimate delights for your millions of sensual receptors! Your hands (which are the most sexually *active* part of your body), are considered by your brain to be the most *important* part of your body. Use them, in conjunction with aromatic oils, and to lead your partner, gently and sensuously, into a state of total arousal. Ideally make sure that the environment, your hands and the oil are warm, and that as with your mouth, your sexual massage covers your lover's entire body.

Caress each other. We normally think of a caress as with the hand or arm. You, as one of the Sexually Intelligent, can use every part of your body to caress that of your partner. Your fingertips and hands can explore all parts of your partner's body. In addition to your hands and mouth you can use other parts of your body to caress, stroke and explore the miracle that is your partner.

Pay special attention to the erogenous zones, which vary from person to person, but which tend to include the mouth, the ears, the neck, the throat, the nipples, the back, the buttocks and the inner thighs.

Now that you have gone through the Brain Workout, just take a few minutes to think about *your* ideal sex partner. Mind Map® your ideal Adonis or Aphrodite – their looks, characteristics, personality, etc. The color plate section has an example of a Sex Partner Mind Map® to help you (plate 7).

SEX AND AGE – SOME GOOD NEWS!

Now that you have nearly completed your multi-intelligence Sexual Brain Workout, let me provide you with some interesting facts on the full nature of sex and age. I have conducted surveys over the last 20 years into public assumptions about sexual activity. The results are surprisingly consistent across languages and cultures, and they indicate that it is generally assumed that from around 60 – and even 50 onwards – there was little sexual activity or drive at all. However, what are the facts?

Numerous studies, including the later studies by Masters and Johnson and the Hite Report, are now revealing that the reality is very different. Sexual activity does not actually decline as people get older, and often couples report that intercourse becomes far more intimate, meaningful and satisfying as they get older. These findings shouldn't be that unexpected though, if you take a minute to think about what actually happens in life.

In their 20s and 30s people are usually busy establishing careers and starting families – and the demands of babies and young children are well-known to drain their parents' energy (not to mention opportunities!). However, by the time the couple have reached their 50s and 60s, their children will usually have established their own homes and families, and with retirement from work comes new freedom and time for the couple to spend time enjoying each other's company again. Individuals are also far more sexually experienced, considerate and aware than when they were younger, which means that lovemaking, instead of consisting of the rushed physical urgencies of younger generations, can be a more drawn-out, exploratory, experimental and romantic affair.

DID YOU KNOW?

More than four million people around the world are making love as you read this.

LOVE AS BRAIN FOOD

Further support for sex-throughout-life comes from the fields of brain and nutritional research.

It has been found that the brain requires four essential "foods" for its survival:

- oxygen
- biological nutrition
- information
- love.

We all know that the brain must have material "foods" for it to function, so oxygen and nutrition are clearly vital. What is frequently not realized is that information and love are also prerequisites for a healthy and active brain. Without these essential elements, the brain will go into decline and die. If you don't believe that love is essential to your brain, think about the devastating *physical* effects you would experience (or have experienced), when the person whom you truly love convinces you, with a few powerful and well-chosen words, that not only do they not love you, but are in fact totally indifferent to your existence. The brain *needs* love, and the physical touching and caressing that accompany it.

The following story confirms this.

American nutritionist William Glasser was feeding rabbits a diet that was particularly high in cholesterol. The purpose of the experiment was to determine appropriate cholesterol levels and to discover what levels would be dangerous – i.e., which would cause unhealthy increases in weight. The rabbits in the experiment lived in a number of communal cages and were all put on the same high-cholesterol diet. It was assumed that all the rabbits would react similarly.

Extraordinarily, all but one of the cages of rabbits performed as expected. The exception contained rabbits that were genetically identical to those in the other cages, yet for some inexplicable reason they remained sleek, slim and healthy while all the rabbits in the other cages gained weight as predicted. Glasser and his colleagues could find no reason for this – all the variables between the cages of rabbits were identical.

Approximately a week later, with the "slimline" rabbits maintaining their svelte condition against all predictions, while consuming the high-cholesterol diet, one of the researchers happened to be passing the research lab late at night, when he saw the light on. On investigation, he found one of the night researchers holding one of the renegade rabbits. When asked what she was doing, she explained that the night shift often became very boring and, as she was fond of rabbits, she would give herself a break and spend five or ten minutes stroking and playing with the rabbits in this particular cage.

The experiment provided a stunning, totally unpredicted result. As Dr Glasser succinctly put in his conclusion to the research: *"Eat what you like, but get a little loving every day!"*

ATTITUDE (MIND-SET)

We can now see that sex-through-the-decades is not doomed to an inevitable decline. It is a field of endless opportunity, enjoyment and infinite possibilities for learning and sharing human intimacies with others.

When you carry into the sexual arena – no matter what your age – a body that is beautifully fit, a mind that is intelligent, creative, agile and alert, and an attitude that is constantly curious, open, exploratory, childlike, romantic and concerned, then your sex life and partnerships will be ones of growing ecstasy.

As you have probably gathered, sex is primarily a brain function! It gives you the "play" of *all* your Multiple Intelligences, strengthens your immune system, increases the supply of oxygen and energy to your brain, and in the short, medium and long-term meanings of the phrase, keeps you alive. Cherish it!

Next is your Sexual Intelligence Questionnaire. Remember that a score of 50 per cent or more means that you are doing truly well. A score of 100 per cent means that you are a genius in this intelligence. Check yourself over time and enter your scores in the table on page **221**.

MULTIPLE INTELLIGENCE TEST – SEXUAL INTELLIGENCE

For each of the following questions rank yourself on a scale of 0–100. A score of 0 indicates that the statement is totally untrue; a score of 100 shows that the statement describes you perfectly.

I am completely uninhibited in my sexual activities and life.   SCORE ......

I am a sexually creative lover, using my creativity in all aspects of lovemaking, including preparation, sexual positions and sexual locations, etc. I love thinking of new ways of pleasing my partner.   SCORE ......

I keep my body physically healthy so that it will both appeal to my partner and be able to perform well in the sexual arena.   SCORE ......

Sight is a major sexual stimulant for me, and I play to this sense.   SCORE ......

Hearing is a major sexual stimulant for me, and I play to this sense.   SCORE ......

Smell is a major sexual stimulant for me, and I play to this sense.   SCORE ......

Touch is a major sexual stimulant for me, and I play to this sense.   SCORE ......

I am romantic in all senses of the word.   SCORE ......

I consider sex a wonderful playground, with an emphasis on the word *play*. I often laugh during lovemaking.   SCORE ......

I consider words to be part of my sexual attraction, and use them to romance and seduce my partner.   SCORE ......

I have many and varied sexual fantasies. I love them!   SCORE ......

I consider sex to be a major and important part of my life.   SCORE ......

I consider foreplay to be a significant part of the sexual "game."   SCORE ......

I let my partner know, in various ways, what my likes and preferences are.   SCORE ......

I consider sex and sexual activity a natural and healthy part of human life.   SCORE ......

TOTAL SCORE ......

NOTES

Traditional IQ was seen, throughout the 20th century, as "the" intelligence. The *only* intelligence. We now realize that Traditional Intelligence itself can be broken down into three different intelligences: Numerical, Spatial and Verbal. These three intelligences are also themselves realized to be part of a much greater set of intelligences – the ones you have been learning about.

Part 3 introduces, explores and will help you develop your Traditional IQ. However, first is a little bit about how such a measure of intelligence came to be used in the first place.

the traditional IQ intelligences

At the beginning of the last century, a French psychologist, by the name of Alfred Binet, worked out the first scientific methods for getting an "objective" measure of raw intelligence. His test was simple but elegant. Because at that time it was still thought that intelligence was only connected to words and numbers, Binet set vocabulary and numerical tests to large numbers of children. In each category, he calculated the average score, and gave that score an IQ of 100 – a normal or standard IQ. Any child who did better than average was given a score ranging from 110–200; any child doing worse than average was given a score of 90 or below. The higher or lower scores depended on just *how* far above or below the average the child was.

It is interesting to note that Binet did not devise IQ tests, as many people thought, to damn a child forever to a given score. He did it to *liberate* children. Binet had noticed that poor children, no matter how bright they were, were never given the privilege of further education. Binet thought that if poor children could prove, through an IQ score, that they were brighter than average, then they would be able to get an advanced education, regardless of their social standing.

These IQ tests, which did indeed give millions of children an opportunity they might never have had, were accepted without question until the 1970s. By then it was becoming apparent that, although the tests were originally supposed to give *absolute* scores (i.e., that did not change throughout the child's life), IQ *could* be nurtured and developed.

This is what you will be doing over the next three chapters!

count on
yourself

your numerical intelligence

NUMERICAL INTELLIGENCE - A DEFINITION

Of all the intelligences, Numerical Intelligence is the one that produces the most fear, the most negative reactions, and it is the one which most people rank as their weakest area of ability. Phrases like "I don't like math!," "I can't do math!" and "I never *could* do math, and never *will* be able to do math!" are common.

So just what *is* this magical and mysterious intelligence?

Your Numerical Intelligence is your brain's ability to juggle with the "alphabet" of numbers. One of the mistakes many people make when starting to learn about numbers is thinking that there are millions and millions and limitless *billions* of numbers they have to learn. In fact there are only *ten* numbers to learn: 1, 2, 3, 4, 5, 6, 7, 8, 9 and 0! All the others are simply juggled combinations of these.

And so all you have to do to become Numerically Intelligent is to grasp this fact, and then learn some very simple operations.

DID YOU KNOW?

Most people think that Numerical Intelligence is a gift – you either have it or you don't. Wrong! *Everybody* has the gift; it is simply a matter of unwrapping it.

On the simplest level, numbers help us to define who we are. Each of us is a human being, with **one** heart, **one** head, **one** nose, **one** mouth, **two** eyes, **two** ears, **two** legs, **two** feet, **two** hands, **ten** fingers, **ten** toes and a **million million** brain cells!

Your Numerical Intelligence helps you every single day of your life, and in nearly all of your common activities. Take a few moments to think where the use of numbers – adding, subtracting, multiplying and dividing them – contribute to our everyday activities, such as cooking, shopping, operating the video/television/computer, driving, time-management, vacation planning, study, any sports activity, etc.

Numbers, perhaps without you even knowing it, are something you have been having a love affair with for most of your life!

WHAT'S IN IT FOR YOU?

You will learn how to overcome any lingering fears you may have of numbers, and some simple and easy techniques for helping you to add, subtract, divide and multiply. With just 10 basic units and a few simple formulas, you can play infinite games!

In addition, you will be given all the basic information you need to handle numbers in your everyday life, including a complete formula for getting your finances in order. This will enable you to plan your future so that your money and wealth multiply rather than falling to zero or below!

A NUMERICAL INTELLIGENCE STAR

Cambridge mathematician Andrew Wiles shot to fame in 1994 by finally setting out a proof of a 350-year old mathematical problem, after eight years' work. Wiles first came across Fermat's Last Theorem when he was browsing in a library, aged 10. Then and there, he dreamed of solving it: *"Since I met Fermat's Last Theorem as a child it's been my greatest passion."* It was a passion that dominated the next 30 years of his life.

In the 17th century, Pierre de Fermat, the inventor of analytical geometry and one of the creators of modern number theory, scribbled the following proposition in his notebook:

"X[n+]Y[n+] = Z[n+] has no rational solution for numbers greater than 2" adding in the margin that he did not have "time and paper" to show his "truly marvelous demonstration!" Unfortunately, if Fermat did ever find the time and paper to demonstrate his proof of the proposition, that paper was subsequently lost – and a legend was created. This deceptively simple equation baffled the best mathematical and scientific brains for generations, and its solution by Wiles represents one of the most significant developments in mathematics in the 20th century.

The solution to Fermat's Theorem took a mathematical genius, together with perseverance, determination and lots of Creatively Intelligent day-dreaming. Wiles thought about the problem for 30 years, and the answer only came after dedicating seven entire years exclusively to finding the proof. However, one final cruel hurdle had to be overcome: Wiles announced that he had solved Fermat's Last Theorem, to great acclaim, only for he himself to discover a flaw in that proof. Showing incredible self-belief and Personal Intelligence, he went back to his blackboards. Fourteen months later, Wiles had repaired the proof, and in August 1994, Fermat's Last Theorem was officially solved!

Let's get back to the general "fear and loathing" of mathematics. There are several reasons why these damaging attitudes arise. Fortunately they are *nothing* to do with your basic ability, which we know from everything you have been able to accomplish in your life so far, is superb.

One reason has to do with the timing and order in which you were taught mathematics, and the whole attitude towards "work." This is best illustrated by the story of Oliver, a five-year-old child who, like you, was a potential mathematical prodigy.

Gerard, a mathematician, musician, code-breaker and poet, had brought up his five-year-old son Oliver to adore mathematics. They constantly played mathematical games together, and young Oliver was learning to speak "mathematise" with a facility that was approaching his level of competence in English.

However, when Oliver returned from his first day at school, his attitude had been changed. Gerard asked him, "Did you do mathematics?"

"Yes," came the surly reply.
"And …?" Gerard asked.
"I don't like math!"
Gently, Gerard asked "Why don't you like math?"
Oliver thought for a moment and then replied: "Because of work."
Intrigued by this answer, Gerard asked the next probing and appropriate question: "What's work, then?"
At this, Oliver frowned deeply, thought for a considerable time and finally said: "*Work is doing what you want to do when you don't want to do it.*"
It turned out that his teacher had forbidden Oliver to do mathematics in the morning when he

had wanted to, and had forced him to do mathematics at what was, for him, a boringly simple level in the afternoon, when he did not want to.

Oliver, like many people, had failed to make the distinction between the subject and the situation. The truth of the matter was that he still, deeply and inherently, loved mathematics. What he did *not* like was the situation in which he had been placed to *learn* mathematics, and the person who had forced him into that situation.

Dangerously and unwittingly, young Oliver had lumped one "like" (math) and two "dislikes" (situation and teacher) into one general "don't like" of mathematics.

Another reason why the majority of people are afraid of and don't like numbers relates to the unique way in which mathematics is taught in schools. Mathematics, unlike (for example), geography, is linearly progressive. Geography can be seen as a giant jigsaw puzzle in which you have to fill in all the pieces. If at any time you can't fit in (i.e., don't understand) a piece, it doesn't really matter – you can wait and fill it in later.

Mathematics, on the other hand, is more like building a house of cards. Each card *must* be in place before the next one is added. If any card is misplaced, the entire structure tends to collapse.

For this reason it is *much* easier to "trip up" in mathematics. You have *thousands* of "opportunities" to have the card-house collapse all around you. Most people take those opportunities!

The first and often fatal mistake occurs at the very first stages of learning fundamental addition and subtraction. Often, while the teacher is explaining in detail these basic operations, the young future hater-of-mathematics is looking out of the window of the classroom, day-dreaming about flying with the birds who are etching beautiful (mathematical!) patterns in the sky.

When the result of the first math test is revealed, the young child, despite having missed the basics, still understands the mathematical nature and social and academic significance of zero-out-of-25!

Once again, as was the case for Oliver, the child will base an understandable dislike of the subject on this experience. Once again, like Oliver, the child is compounding positives and negatives into one negative. In this instance it is the love of mathematics (as evidenced by the delight of the flight patterns of the birds), confused with the dislike of failure and humiliation associated with the subject.

MATH LOVE-IN!

We *all*, deep down, love numbers. They help us survive. They reward us. They help us discriminate. They help us rate, rank and compare. They help us explore the universe. And they provide us with limitless hours of games, entertainment and fun.

We all like to be told we are the **One.** We all celebrate when our child, friend, or team comes **first.** We all like to know that our own favorite song/piece of music has entered the **Top 10.** We would all like to be told that we have just won **two million dollars.** We all like to know that the temperature is going to be exactly the **number of degrees** that we find most pleasant. We are all thrilled when some fellow human establishes a **new record.** Many of us are obsessed with the numerical measurements of the human body – **bust, chest, waist and hip size,** as well as with **height, weight and calories.** And increasingly we all read and relish those newspapers, magazines and screen print-outs that give us statistical feedback on all our interests and concerns.

We all love numbers. What has happened to many of us in the past is that we have experienced an unrequited or even punishing love affair! This chapter is designed to get that delightful romance back on track.

It's time to try the Brain Workout.

THE BRAIN WORKOUT – DEVELOPING YOUR NUMERICAL INTELLIGENCE

There are numerous (!) ways for you to improve your Numerical Intelligence.

1. Estimate

Studies of the great mathematical geniuses reveal that they kept their Mathematical Mental Muscles in shape by always *estimating* first, then *calculating* and finally *checking*. Practicing estimation uses the giant super computer your brain has for constantly estimating the probabilities of your survival. Using it will pay you big dividends! Don't automatically reach for that calculator!

2. Learn From Others – Real Life Numbers

In every social group there are people who are amazing with numbers, but who think they are not, simply because *they* know someone who is better ! In a bar one day I was sitting with someone who had a degree in mathematics. He was watching six darts players, each of whom was counting, with lightning speed, their total remaining target score and then multiple divisible ways in which that score could be broken down to give them the fewest remaining necessary darts. He tried to keep up with them and was totally flummoxed! When buying them a drink afterwards, he asked how much training they had had in mathematics. Every single one of them had failed the subject in school! If they had been given grades for *real-life* mathematics, they would have all got straight As!

Similarly people who follow sports like football or baseball will often claim that they are no good at maths, while being able to recite reams of data and statistics on their favourite teams and players. Anyone who is interested in the standing of their team, or the average scoring rate of a particular player, has a brain that is naturally inclined towards an intelligence numerically!

DID YOU KNOW?

Simply by training his memory, someone was able to memorize a "telephone number" 42,195 digits long.

Whenever you find *anyone* who seems to be good at *any* aspect of calculating with numbers, ask them how they do it. You will find that most of them love to explain, and usually transfer their knowledge to your brain extremely well and quickly!

3. Beat the Odds

For many people statistics, probabilities and, especially, odds are particularly frightening, because it seems that they contain millions of numbers. In fact odds are quite simple, and you can calculate them quite easily. For example, if you want to calculate the odds on winning the Lottery, simply find out how many rows of numbers have been selected. If it is 10 million, then your chance of winning the top prize is one chance in 10 million. If 100 winners are going to be selected for the second prize, then your chance of winning is 100 divided into 10 million, which gives you one chance in 100,000.

Using your right-brain imagination, you can "picture" this chance. The chance of winning the second prize would be the chance of being selected as the only person out of a completely full football stadium; the chance of winning the first prize would be equal to being the only person selected out of the entire population of a city the size of London or New York.

4. Ranking

One of the great strengths of numbers is that they can help you to rank, organize and analyze information, especially information about yourself. When your brain is able to do this, it can see a much clearer picture of what is going on, and can adjust its behaviour towards its desired goals.

The following simple exercise will help to explain this more easily!

How you Spend your Time – Ideal vs. Reality

Below is a list of activities, between which most of us tend to divide our time. Rank them from 1–8 in order of the amount of time each activity takes up during a typical week. The most time-consuming rank number 1, the least number 8 (you may want to refer to the Time Juggler Mind Map® on plate 3 again):

- work
- education
- sleep
- social life/friends
- children
- partner
- other family
- holidays/days off.

Next, estimate the amount of your time that you spend on each activity during a typical week out of a total of 100 – the percentage of your time spent each week on each activity; note it down.

Now rank the list again, in the order of time priority that you would like the activities to be in your life, in your ideal world!, and put down the percentage of time that you would like each to take up in your ideal week.

Having done this, the real and ideal can be compared. Below, note down your time priority order of activities in your ideal order. Place your ideal percentage next to it in the "Ideal" column; then place your real percentage in the "Real" column. Finally, subtract the "Real" from the "Ideal" and place the answer in the "Difference" column. For example, if for "Social life/friends" your

"Ideal" percentage was 20 per cent and your "Real" 8 per cent, the difference would be 12 per cent.

Activity	Ideal	Real	Difference

Using numbers for ranking, analyzing and organizing your life is useful both in the results that it achieves, and because, as you do it, it exercises and strengthens your "mathematical muscles."

5. Beat the Calculator

The calculator can destroy your mathematical muscle or make it stronger. I once saw a brilliant mathematician automatically tap into his calculator, to which he had become addicted, 2 + 2!

Don't use your calculator as a crutch! Use it, instead, as a training device and companion. Use your growing ability to estimate, and see how often you can come up with an answer that is "in the right ball park" before you have even started to use the calculator. Similarly if a friend or co-worker is using a calculator for some addition or estimation, see if you can beat them to the correct answer or approximation. As you improve your skill (and it *will* improve) accelerate your speed – another significant factor in improving your mathematical intelligence.

6. Play Mental Calculation Games

This is something that mathematical geniuses regularly practice to keep their mathematical muscles toned.

Start with some simple additions, subtractions, divisions and multiplications, such as 4 + 5; 8 − 3; 6 ÷ 2; and 2 x 4. Gradually build these up until you are comfortable with first two and then three digit numbers. Try the examples below to get you started.

81 + 34 =
56 + 13 =
683 + 725 =
497 + 365 =
892 + 457 =

84 − 43 =
22 − 14 =
487 − 86 =
765 − 94 =
462 − 321 =

93 ÷ 3 =
86 ÷ 4 =
49 ÷ 7 =
60 ÷ 5 =
160 ÷ 8 =

68 x 4 =
32 x 8 =
13 x 9 =
27 x 12 =
17 x 16 =

7. Mathematical Super Techniques

No.1 – Knowing you Can

Those who are excellent with numbers make up "speed calculation" techniques that help them accelerate their calculating speed, improve their accuracy and, therefore, raise their Numerical Intelligence. The first "technique" they use will be simply to realize that they *can* develop and use special techniques to help them calculate far faster than average. By the time you have tried the following, *you will know too*!

No.2 – Subtracting from 100, 1000, 10,000, 100,000 and 1,000,000

Surprisingly, you can do this easily in your head if you do exactly the *opposite* of what you were probably taught in school! Instead of working from right to left, you work from left to right.

Starting with the number at the furthest left, you subtract it, and each subsequent number as you move to the right, from nine. The last, and *only* the last, digit you subtract from 10.

For example, if you wanted to subtract 58 from 100, you would subtract 5 from 9 giving you 4, and 8 from 10 giving you 2, and hey presto! The correct answer is 42.

It's just as simple with a million. If you wanted to subtract 795,238 from 1,000,000, you subtract 7 from 9 = 2, then 9 from 9 = 0, then 5 from 9 = 4, and 2 from 9 = 7, then 3 from 9 = 6, and finally 8 from 10 = 2 – giving you the correct answer: 204,762.

Imagine if you had been able to do this when you were in school ...

If you *really* want to stun people, ask them to write down a number in the billions and tell them that you can subtract it from 10 billion without using pen or paper and reciting your answer, as soon as you have seen the question, at standard dictation speed. They (and you) will be stunned by your genius!

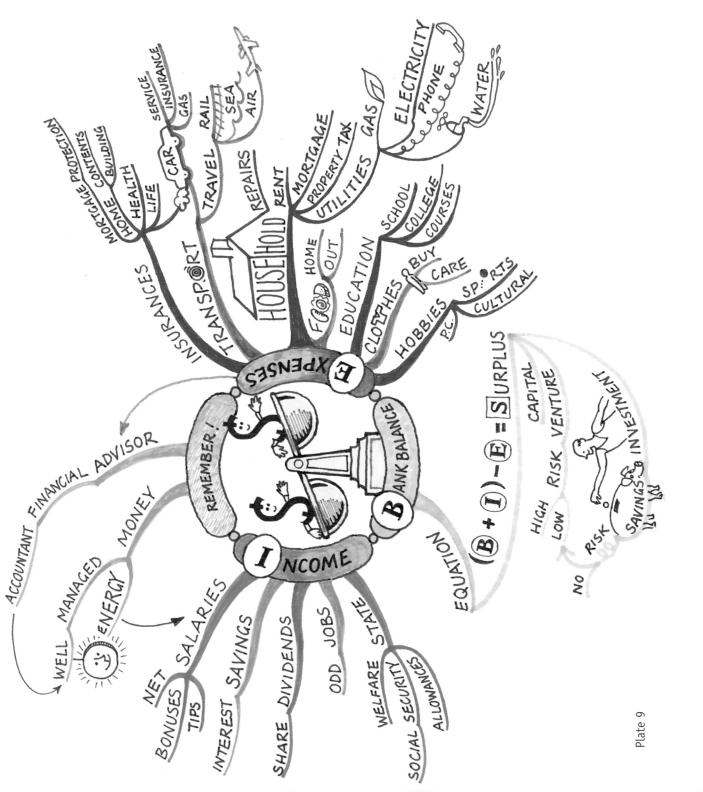

Plate 9

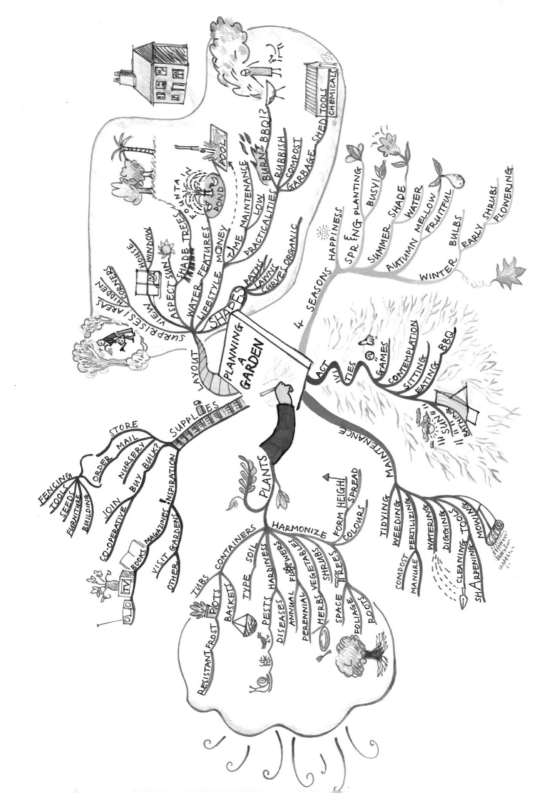

PLANNING A GARDEN

Plate 10

No.3 - Adding in 10 Packets

When adding columns of figures, quickly check to see if there are any "10 packets" that can help accelerate your progress (a "packet" is any combination of numbers that go to make up 10; for example 5 + 5; 3 + 7; 3 + 2 + 5; 2 + 2 + 5 + 1; 2 + 2 + 2 + 2 + 2; etc.). For example, in the following column:

69

37

51

22

93

16

74

58

85

45

it would be a waste of your time, and an inappropriate use of your mathematical mental muscle, to start as most people do, mumbling to yourself "9 + 7 = 16 + 1 = 17 + 2 = 19 + 3 = 22 + 6 = 28 ... " Far better to scan quickly for the "10 packets," and add *them* up. This technique can often make you *twice as fast* when adding columns of numbers together.

No.4 - Multiplying Numbers by 11

To multiply any two-digit number by 11, simply add the two digits together and put their sum in the middle of them.

For example, if you want to multiply 53 x 11, add 5 + 3 to give you 8, place it in between the 5 and the 3, giving you 583 as the correct answer.

If the sum of two digits comes to 10 or more, simply add this number to the left digit. For example, if you wanted to multiply 97 x 11, you would add the 9 and 7 to give you 16, put the 6 in the middle and add the 1 to the 9, giving you the correct answer of 1067.

No.5 – Division by 5

To divide any number by 5, which can be quite complex, you can make it incredibly simple by first dividing by 10, and then multiplying by 2.

For example, if you want to divide 2,340 by 5, you would simply knock off the last digit, and then multiply the remaining ones by 2, giving you the correct answer of 468.

8. Memory Techniques

Good mathematicians memorize numbers easily by "chunking" them. If someone gives you a telephone number 8496063, break it into chunks of 3 and 4 digits, thus giving you 2 instead of 7 "bits" to remember ("849" ... "6063" is much easier to remember than the entire number right off). Also, to make the memory even more secure in your head, listen to the rhythm or music of the particular number, and see if there are any interesting relationships in it. For example, the last 4-digit chunk is composed of two 60s plus 3.

A particularly good technique for remembering telephone numbers is to chunk them as above, and also to remember the rhythm and "shape" of the number on the phone dialling pad. This technique will also help increase your Spatial Intelligence (*see Chapter 9*).

9. Mind Sports and Games

Mind sport games, such as backgammon and bridge, are very good for increasing your powers of ongoing estimation and calculation, and players of these games often report big improvements in their general ability with numbers. Pool and darts are also good games for increasing numerical ability.

10. Everyday Numbers

Become increasingly aware of just how good you already are with numbers, and how much you use them in your daily life and everyday actions. You work out, almost without thinking, how much time is left before lunch, before work is over, to the break, the date, the end of the game ... You constantly check to see that you have the right change; you calculate at the checkout which is the best queue to choose; you shop for clothes based on the constant or changing sizes of the various bits of your body; you know in a flash which is the largest piece of pie!

You are a walking mathematical genius. Simply become aware of it, and train that amazing ability to become even more powerful.

case study

One of the greatest Numerical Intelligences in recent times was Alan Turing. He accomplished two major feats, either one of which would have been a lifetime achievement for anyone.

During the Second World War Turing was one of an élite band of civilians who worked at Britain's secret code-breaking establishment at Bletchley Park. The job of these people (recruited from the top universities and for their abilities in solving mind games like chess and crosswords) was to intercept and decode the Germans' encrypted radio transmissions. The Germans had developed a coding machine (the Enigma machine) which was capable of 159 *trillion* different settings. Turing and a young history student, Harry Hinsley, played a huge part in the eventual decoding of the "unbreakable" Enigma Code in August 1941, which undoubtedly helped to shorten the war, and saved many, many lives.

Still in love with numbers and mathematics, and still bursting for new challenges, Turing toyed with the creation of a little mathematical gadget for all of us to play with. He invented the computer.

FINANCIAL SELF-MANAGEMENT

The area where the most fear about numbers is generally experienced is that of financial self-management. Many people get into trouble because they are reluctant to look at their financial facts. They assume that things will generally sort themselves out, but live in constant fear of bills, credit card statements, and those unexpected expenses that can strike out of the blue. It doesn't matter if you are comfortably off either – even people earning large salaries can invite disaster through inadequate financial planning.

The art of budgeting should be an essential part of your self-management system. Budgeting is actually quite simple, once you get the hang of organizing yourself and your finances systematically, and if you make sure that you know roughly when you will receive any money coming to you (your wages, any dividends from stocks and shares you may have, maintenance money, etc.), and when you have to pay your regular bills. To help you consider all of the aspects of budgeting, have a look at the Budgeting Mind Map®, color plate 9. This sort of planning can be expanded to cover an entire year, when it is called "cash flow forecasting." A cash flow forecast will enable you to plan more consciously just where, and when, you wish to spend your money.

If you have not already done any basic financial analysis of your own situation, try the following exercise.

Cash Flow Forecasts

On the opposite page is a 12-month cash flow sheet, which will allow you to work out your first rough forecast.

Cash Flow Forecast											For the period From _____ To _____	Total for whole period
Month												
Income sources												
Total income for period **A**												
Expenditure												
Total expenditure for period **B**												
Difference between **A** and **B**												

In the top section, make a note of the various sources of income you have, for each month, and when you *expect to receive* your income. For example, interest on a savings account may be paid twice a year during each September and April. Therefore you should remember to add an estimate of this amount of interest into your income total for these months. Add up your total income for the period.

Next, consider your expenditure for each month. This should include regular items such as rent or mortgage payments, heating, power and telephone bills, commuting expenses, etc., as well as expected "one-off" expenses like holidays or car insurance. When you have completed all your entries, add up your expenses for each month. Then for each month calculate the difference between your income and expenditure.

Annual income twenty pounds, annual expenditure nineteen nineteen six, result happiness. Annual income twenty pounds, annual expenditure twenty pounds ought and six, result misery. (*David Copperfield*, Charles Dickens)

Managing your money in an organized fashion like this will allow you to feel more in control of your finances. You will be able to see where possible "cash flow shortages" might arise (before they hit you!), and so give yourself a bit of time to plan a way round them (maybe by saving a bit of money beforehand, or arranging a loan to cover yourself).

Alternatively, you may find that you have, or are going to have, a certain amount of money left over. Such a surplus would enable you to decide the best time to buy things (for example, in end-of-year sales, etc.). It could also enable you to save regularly for the future, such as putting money aside in a pension plan or for a holiday.

Here is your Numerical Intelligence Questionnaire. Remember that a score of 50 per cent or more means that you are doing truly well. A score of 100 per cent means that you are a numerical genius. Check yourself over time, and enter your scores on the table on page **221**.

MULTIPLE INTELLIGENCE TEST – NUMERICAL INTELLIGENCE

For each question rank yourself on a scale of 0–100. A score of 0 would mean that the statement in no way whatsoever applies to you; a score of 50 that it is half-true; and a score of 100 that it describes you perfectly.

I use numbers and calculations regularly in my daily life. SCORE ......

I have a wide range of skills with numbers and can use all the basic numerical transactions with ease. SCORE ......

I like numbers and anything to do with them. SCORE ......

People often comment on my facility with numbers. SCORE ......

In school I consistently achieved high marks in mathematics and physics. SCORE ......

I love to play mathematical games and solve mathematical puzzles. SCORE ......

I have a good memory for numbers including telephone numbers and important dates. SCORE ......

Numbers to me have different personalities: I sometimes see them with their very own specific colors and unique shapes, and have emotional feelings for and reactions to them. SCORE ......

I prefer to work out basic numerical problems in my head rather than using a calculator. SCORE ......

TOTAL SCORE ......

As a little extra, here is another short Numerical/Mathematical Intelligence test for you to do. (The answers are on page **176**.) Once again, repeat this test over a period of time, and watch your score rise as your Numerical Intelligence increases.

NUMERICAL/MATHEMATICAL TEST

1 Insert the missing number: (50 points)

   14, 17, 20, 23, ...

2 Insert the missing number: (50 points)

   93, 85, 77, 69, ...

3 Fill in the missing number: (100 points)

1	12	12
3	4	12
10	20	?

4 What is the missing number?   (100 points)

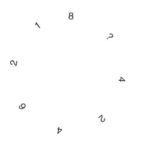

5 Fill in the missing number: (100 points)

   I N T 5 LL I – 5 N T

6   Fill in the next number: (100 points)

1, 4, 8, 13, 19, 26, ...

7   Insert the missing number: (150 points)

16	11	25	14	16	5
	9		13		?

8   Insert the missing number: (100 points)

1	4	8	2
6	5	3	10
4	3	?	8

9   Find the missing number: (150 points)

37	13	5	3
	25	9	?

10 What is the next number in this series?   (100 points)

9, 11, 21, 23, 33, 35, ...

TOTAL SCORE ......

ANSWERS – Numerical/Mathematical Intelligence Test

1 23 (they each increase by three)

2 69 (they each decrease by eight)

3 200 (the figure in the left-hand column is multiplied by the figure in the centre column to give the figure in the right-hand column)

4 3 or 12 (each pair of diagonally opposite numbers is made up of a half and a double)

5 7 (this question decodes into A = 1, B = 2, C = 3, etc. The word thus spells INTELLIGENT, with G (7) as the missing letter)

6 34 (each one is increased by one more than the previous number)

7 7 (add the numbers at top right and top left, and divide by three: $16 + 5 = 21 \div 3 = 7$)

8 6 (each horizontal row has two numbers that are half the other two)

9 4 (numbers in the lower row were obtained by halving the total of the two above them)

10 45 (add 2 and 10 alternately)

NOTES

mind the gap

your spatial intelligence

SPATIAL INTELLIGENCE - A DEFINITION

Spatial Intelligence is the second of the three pillars of the standard IQ tests. Like Numerical Intelligence, it is one in which many people consider themselves particularly weak, or a talent that some people have and most do not! However, Spatial Intelligence, just like *all* intelligences, can be explained, understood *and* developed.

Your Spatial Intelligence is your ability to see the relationships of shapes to each other, and to see the relationship of things in space. This intelligence also includes the ability of your body to negotiate successfully the environment and world around you. It involves your ability to read a map too, and to translate the information from that map into correct actions in the area.

By the very fact that you are still alive, we know you must be more intelligent than any of the world's most powerful computers in this area of genius.

Think about how you use this intelligence when you walk from room to room in your house, when you set the table, cross the road, arrange or rearrange things in your home, walk down the street, ride your bike, drive your car, and play any sport. As you can see, this intelligence is directly and intimately connected to your Physical Intelligence. Improve one and you will automatically improve the other.

WHAT'S IN IT FOR YOU?

By the time you have finished this chapter and emerged from your Brain Workout, you will realize that your own Spatial Intelligence is already incredibly well developed. You will know why soccer players are by no means "stupid," and will also know how it is that London taxi drivers develop brains that are physically bigger than the average person's! This isn't all – you will have learnt basic techniques for improving your standard IQ scores, and will also know how to find yourself when you have become lost, as well as how not to get lost so often!

A SPATIAL INTELLIGENCE STAR

Our next intelligence star is one who uses his Spatial Intelligence for hours on end in death-defying situations. If he uses it well, he lives to use it another day. If it fails him, he dies.

Who is he? Formula One Motor Racing Champion, Michael Schumacher.

Just consider what he has to do. For hours on end Schumacher has to drive his car immaculately at speeds ranging from 50 to over 200 miles per hour; be aware of every other car that is hurtling around him at its own shifting and different speeds; note the surface of the track, and depending on its temperature and dampness adjust everything accordingly; observe the fantastically rapidly shifting scenery before his eyes, and calculate in advance the actions he will have to take to negotiate it successfully; feel the change in the weight of his car as his gas is used up, and change both his steering and his speed in order to compensate; similarly feel the changing nature of his tires, and calculate what adjustments he needs to make when cornering at breakneck speed; be on the constant look out for changing signs at the side of the track, possible oil slicks, and wrecked cars ahead of him, all of which may require dramatic avoidance action; and, when overtaking, to calculate the angles, curves, speeds and velocities that may either win or lose him the race, or save or lose him his life.

Schumacher has put his considerable Spatial Intelligence to good use. Already his superb spatial and tactical thinking, along with what has been called his "unbelievable" car control, have made him the youngest double World Champion in the sport's history. He is thought to be worth around a second per lap over the world's other drivers in ordinary race conditions, and in a league of his own in the wet!

But Schumacher's Spatial Intelligence is not the only one he has developed. His Physical Intelligence is phenomenal (it has to be for him to stand the physical demands of his sport!), and he has tremendous self-belief and confidence.

Top candidates for professions and hobbies requiring super Spatial Intelligence:

- sky divers
- trapeze artists
- gymnasts
- iceskaters
- soccer players.

Spatial Intelligence enables you to think about the intricate interrelationships in the world of three dimensions. This intelligence can involve wide spaces, such as those required of the astronomer, the sailor or the airline pilot, or the more local spaces of the painter, the team-playing athlete, the architect, the sculptor, the mechanical engineer or the surgeon.

However, Spatial Intelligence is one in which many people rate themselves low. Why? It is usually because they have had experiences in geometry similar to those experienced by the "math-haters" of Chapter 8. Or they have had embarrassing spatial experiences in sports, where they have failed to place the ball where it needed to be.

But statements such as "I can't do geometry" or "I have no sense of space or direction" *cannot* be true: just consider what your brain does on a normal day.

YOUR BRAIN'S DAILY SPATIAL GENIUS STORY

The following story looks at this from your brain-as-a-massive-bio-computer point of view. As you read, try to guess what activity is being described.

Wanting to approach a horizontal line that theoretically stretches to infinity in both directions, your super bio-computer manipulates an unbelievably complex system composed of millions of levers and pulleys, and directs them through three-dimensional space to that desired line.

Your super bio-computer then swivels to the left, and takes in, at billions of units of information per second, the entire three-dimensional plane before it. It notices hundreds of three-dimensional objects, of different sizes and of every imaginable shape and color. A few are not moving. Most are. Those that are moving are moving in different directions and are of multiple sizes, masses and shapes. Each one is travelling at its own unique velocity.

In a split second your super bio-computer registers this entire geometry-in-motion scene and extrapolates precisely where every moving object will be within the next two-to-five seconds. It then swivels to the right, and with an entirely new three-dimensional vista composed of its own static and moving multi-varied geometric shapes, performs exactly the same kind of geometric calculations and predictions.

Having completed these immensely complex calculations, matched them together, swivelled to the left to double check that all the multi-billion facets of reality are acting as they were predicted to do, your super bio-computer instructs the million-fold system of levers and pulleys to dance through the moving geometric shapes that arc hurtling across the three-dimensional plane your brain wishes to traverse.

Having successfully completed this action, your bio-computer brain then manipulates the lever/pulley system perfectly into one of the more rectangular geometric structures, and by subtle manipulation engineers it to move among the to-and-froing geometric landscape.

Your super bio-computer brain then unerringly manipulates its own three-dimensional cube through tens to hundreds of miles of geometric space, magically avoiding any contact with the tens of thousands of objects that are coming at it from all directions, and at infinitely different angles and varying speeds.

Throughout this entire time your super bio-computer brain has monitored and negotiated symbols, signals, flashing lights, sounds, right angles, circles and semi-circles, gradients and innumerable impediments and obstacles.

Upon reaching its destination, millions of such super bio-computer brains have been known, inexplicably, to exclaim "I can't do math!"

Having just done what?!

Having just completed a non-stop series of billion-faceted geometric and algebraic equations with unerring accuracy! And all in aid of what? The common daily routine of walking across a busy street, getting into your car and driving home!

Your day-to-day accomplishments in simply surviving this geometric world in which we live demonstrate that you are, by nature, a genius in the arts and sciences of geometry and spatial awareness.

DID YOU KNOW?

Using your brain actually makes it grow bigger!

THE LONDON CABBY STORY

A wonderful piece of new brain research recently confirmed that developing your Spatial Intelligence is not only possible; when you do it increases the size of your brain!

A study carried out found that London taxi drivers' brains physically expand as they complete "the Knowledge" (the memorization of the complete map of London), and that the longer they have been driving a taxi, the bigger that special part of their brain which controls navigation is likely to grow! This area of the brain is known as the hippocampus and deals with the storage of memories, mapping, and Engineering Intelligence. It continues to get bigger as the cabbies absorb experience and knowledge as they navigate around the city.

As soon as the findings were published, a local newspaper decided to pit a London cabby against an in-car satellite guidance system, a laptop running the latest route-finding software, and the *A-Z Map of London*. The challenge was to drive, finding the best and fastest route, from a pre-determined spot in the city centre to a location in North West London.

The result?

- The cabby's completion time: 33 minutes
- The in-car satellite guidance system: 55 minutes
- The *A-Z of London*: 60 minutes ·
- Laptop route-finding software: 70 minutes

The human brain wins again!

DID YOU KNOW?

By walking down a crowded street, you are doing something that none of the world's most powerful and advanced computers can even *begin* to do!

Knowing now that you have this gigantic Spatial Intelligence at your command, it's time to take it for a good workout!

BRAIN WORKOUT – DEVELOPING YOUR SPATIAL INTELLIGENCE

1. Play Imagination Games

Albert Einstein, one of the greatest spatial geniuses of all time, used to train his students to develop their Spatial Intelligences by recommending that they play imagination games. Einstein informed them (and the world!) that he considered *"imagination more important than knowledge"* – he considered the imagination to be infinite, whereas knowledge could never be so unless you were God!

Take yourself on increasingly complex imaginary journeys from A to B, using all your senses to help you to remember and explore the different elements on your route. This will establish giant imaginative maps in your brain that will enhance your spatial IQ, and will also improve your creative thinking and memory skills.

2. Play any Board Game

Board games, especially chess and its variations, the Japanese game of Go, the Arabian game of Dama, and the various forms of checkers are terrific ways of improving your Spatial Intelligence. Each requires you to stretch and improve your spatial awareness, while simultaneously improving your analytic and strategic thinking skills.

case study

Garry Kasparov, the World Chess Champion, is a master of Spatial Intelligence. He realizes that chess is not simply a linear number-crunching game; it is a vast universe of billions of different geometric possibilities that all take place in three-dimensional space.

Kasparov can remember, perfectly, thousands of the greatest chess games of history, often being able to identify any given game by one move from the middle of that game!

3. Improving your Ball Game

If you notice, for example, that you are continually hitting the ball out of the tennis court, *don't* get frustrated. Use your Visual and Spatial Intelligences to tell you that you are obviously hitting the ball both with too much force and at too high an angle. Use your Personal Intelligence to calm yourself down, take in the information from your last attempt, and adjust your next try. If you use this approach, your brain will continually calculate its next attempt based on good information from the last attempt. Occasionally it will still go wildly wrong, but as time goes by it will gradually improve – as will everything on which you focus this very adaptable intelligence.

Every athlete is a spatial and mathematical genius. The media labelling of football players as "stupid" and "thick" is to its own discredit, and is in complete ignorance of the fact that the skills such players demonstrate are supreme examples of one of the human brain's most precious intelligences, requiring unique combinations of the mathematics of spatial awareness and agility. Think back to the story of your genius brain on page **182**, and imagine translating the processes described there to a game of football, played in front of millions of people, and you will begin to appreciate just how smart athletes have to be!

4. Try Computer Games

Despite some of their adverse publicity, many of the modern adventure computer games are marvellous at training your spatial awareness in conjunction with your speed of perception and speed of reaction. Games such as Simcity®, which requires you to construct an entire virtual reality city, are particularly good.

Try visiting any games arcade, and challenge your Spatial Intelligence. You will often find players there who have developed their skills to an astonishing level. Exercise your Social Intelligence by complimenting them on their skills, and you may be lucky and get a free lesson!

5. Dancing and Physical Activities

Expand your skills by taking up different forms of dance, including Latin American, line dancing, jazz, disco and ballroom. In addition to giving you a fantastic physical workout, these dances will expand your Spatial Intelligence (and improve your social life).

Regularly engage in physical activities that similarly stretch your spatial awareness. These can include all team sports, skiing, shooting and archery, and cross-country running, etc. The selection is large and tempting!

6. Know Where you Are

When you travel to new environments, immediately establish compass directions and the positions of major rivers, roads, buildings and monuments. These give you a simple matrix from which everything else can be worked out. Your brain is naturally designed to do this as a survival mechanism; it simply needs you to give it the first "stakes" in the ground.

7. Get Unlost!

Many people lose themselves because they fail to take advantage of one Spatial Intelligence technique used by people who have high IQs in this area. That technique is to occasionally look *behind* you as well as in front. When you look behind, checking where you have been, make a note of any outstanding buildings or natural objects, and make sure you locate them in relation to each other.

In this way, when you return you will already have seen and be familiar with the route on the way back. Most of those people who get lost are lost not because they have low Spatial Intelligence, but because they have never seen where they are supposed to go!

8. Learn to Play Pool

This is a game that puts a massive emphasis on your Spatial Intelligence. It is also fun, and in the playing of it you will also sharpen up your mathematical and social skills.

9. Study Basic Astronomy

Get a good idea of the map of the universe. Know the few basic sizes and distances and speeds that cover most of the building blocks of the knowledge of the universe. The numbers are also big enough to help you make comparisons with the power of the intelligences of your brain.

10. Buy Geometric Puzzle/Game Books

These sort of books abound with Spatial Intelligence exercises, and are great to carry around with you to fill in those odd "waiting moments" or to while away the time when on a bus or train.

11. Doodle!

Doodling, which has mistakenly been assumed to demonstrate that you have no powers of concentration, is exactly the opposite. Doodling is the Engineering/Spatial Intelligence within your brain pleading for an opportunity to express itself! Let it out!

12. Have a "Multidimensional Toy"

A "multidimensional toy" such as a Rubik's Cube®, a Lego set or some form of three-dimensional puzzle on your coffeetable or desk, gives your brain the chance to "mess around" in the playground of Spatial Intelligence!

13. Mind Map®!

The Mind Map® technique is a demonstration of Spatial Intelligence writ large! It stimulates your multi-billion photon-receiving eyes by feeding them color, and improves the power of your understanding, concentration and memory by showing how and where things link together in the maps of your thoughts.

Your Spatial Intelligence Questionnaire is next. Remember that a score of 50 per cent or more means that you are doing truly well. A score of 100 per cent means that you are a genius in this intelligence. Check yourself over time to watch your scores rise and enter them on the table on page **221**.

MULTIPLE INTELLIGENCE TEST – SPATIAL INTELLIGENCE

In scoring this test, give yourself 0 if the statement is absolutely untrue, and 100 if it is explosively true.

I enjoy games such as checkers, chess and Go.   SCORE ......

I am good at physical sports that require spatial awareness, such
as baseball, basketball, etc.   SCORE ......

I am one of the best people I know at giving, receiving and
understanding directions.   SCORE ......

I love maps and map reading, and can always translate them
accurately in the real world.   SCORE ......

When I make notes, I always use shapes, colors and diagrams
to help me understand better.   SCORE ......

I love taking things apart – and I can put them back together
again!   SCORE ......

I enjoy games and jigsaw puzzles, especially the three-dimensional
sort.   SCORE ......

I am the person to whom others come when mechanical objects
and other forms of machinery need fixing.   SCORE ......

I am excellent at all forms of arcade and video games.   SCORE ......

I love geometry/mechanical drawing/woodwork/crafts/interior design/graphic art/fine art, etc.   SCORE ......

I am fascinated by astronomy, including the relative distance and position of objects in the universe, and their shapes and structures.   SCORE ......

TOTAL SCORE ......

the power of words

your verbal intelligence

VERBAL INTELLIGENCE - A DEFINITION

Verbal Intelligence is the third of the three "graces" of intelligences that go to make up your traditional IQ score.

No matter what anyone may have told you, you are – by definition – extremely bright in this area.

How do we know this?

Because you have learnt the language you speak! To do this, your brain had to be *far* more intelligent than the world's most intelligent computer. The problem for most of us is, that after the first fantastic burst of learning when we were babies, our development of this intelligence slows down, because we get bored in school and lose interest in the subject, perhaps because some grammatical concepts are presented in difficult ways and we don't see their relevance, or because some poetry seems too complicated and unconnected to our lives.

The development and growth of your Verbal Intelligence has been found to be the biggest single factor that determines your success in school and work, not to mention the rapidly growing "Information Economy." Too many people feel that they cannot really improve their verbal skills – wrong! It is *easy* to become a Verbal Intelligence genius.

WHAT'S IN IT FOR YOU?

In this chapter you will learn how to improve your Verbal Intelligence in easy and enjoyable steps. You will learn how to increase and improve your vocabulary and will have already begun this process by the time you reach the end of the chapter. You will also find out the basic principles behind improving your reading speed and comprehension, and how to develop your logical thinking powers.

Your Verbal Intelligence is based on your ability to juggle the 26 letters of the alphabet, and to rearrange them progressively into words, phrases, sentences, paragraphs, chapters, etc. It is the brain's basic Verbal Intelligence that has created all the thousands of different languages that have been spoken around the world.

DID YOU KNOW?

You only have to learn 1,000 key words to master the basics of a foreign language.

The ability of your brain to use words is a sign, a signal, a manifestation of the fact that you *are* intelligent. The more capable you are of juggling them, using them, seeing different relationships between them, and using a growing number of them, then the more intelligent in this area you are considered to be. Verbal Intelligence is obviously an intelligence that can be developed, and in the Brain Workout later on you will be given some entertaining and fun games and exercises to help you improve this mental skill.

The more you develop the power of your vocabulary, the more your brain is able to distinguish and communicate things in an increasingly refined, sophisticated and meaningful way. Verbal Intelligence is a *major* partner to your Social Intelligence, and it can also be seen as a close friend and companion of your Sensual Intelligence. It is your eyes, ears, nose, mouth and skin that give you all the information that your brain uses to make up words. For example, your eye sees an object and your brain labels it: "rose." We then use these very same words to speak to ourselves and others about our experience of this "rose."

As you set out on the journey of improving your own verbal intelligence, it will be useful to give yourself benchmarks, so that you can see where you stand at the moment, and establish your future goals.

What do you think is the average person's writing vocabulary? Speaking vocabulary? Recognition vocabulary?

The answers are as follows:

- Average writing vocabulary   900–1,000 words
- Average speaking vocabulary   1,000–1,100 words
- Average recognition vocabulary   5,000 words

And, just to put them into context:

- World record holder – Shakespeare   25,000 words!

A VERBAL INTELLIGENCE STAR

Shakespeare's works are generally agreed to be the greatest single achievement in English, or even in world literature.

In his short working life Shakespeare wrote 37 plays, as well as 154 sonnets of exquisite quality and two superb long poems. His plays have been translated into more than 50 languages – more than any other playwright in history – and have become the criterion against which all subsequent drama has been measured.

Shakespeare had an extremely high Creative Intelligence as well, using his incredible word power to convey brilliant new insights and ideas. Because of this fantastic combination, Shakespeare is by far the most quoted writer in the history of the human race. In the *Oxford Dictionary of Quotations*, which contains almost 20,000 quotations, a staggering 65 pages (about 10 per cent of the book!) are devoted to him.

Shakespeare used his growing Verbal Intelligence to read widely. In this way he acquired a vast knowledge of politics, science, classical literature, law, Latin, French, sports, music, history, mathematics, philosophy and the arts – all of which he drew on in his plays.

Despite the fact that Shakespeare's plays are one of the main subjects for high school and university study and examinations, he wrote for a popular audience, and the people who thronged to listen to his brilliant, poetic, witty and often bawdy words were primarily tradespeople, laborers and peasants. One of the reasons for his popularity was that he used his words to explore such wide-ranging and universal subjects as birth, love, lust, deceit, beauty, intrigue, murder, romance, despair and hope – subjects everyone has had experience of and can understand.

You have seen that the average writing and speaking vocabulary is *only* 1,000 words. And so the task of improving it, and your ability to make associations with it, can be seen as a lot easier than it might have at first appeared. You do not have to learn thousands of words to become, suddenly, a literary giant! You need only a few hundred more to make a massive percentage increase in your verbal skills.

THE BRAIN WORKOUT – DEVELOPING YOUR VERBAL INTELLIGENCE

Happily there are many things you can do to improve your Verbal Mental Muscle. All of them give you quick feedback and improvement. All of them are enjoyable!

1. Increase your Vocabulary

This is an easy task and has profound results.

Every day, pick one new word that you wish to add to your vocabulary. The magic trick here is to use it, in different contexts, between 5 and 10 times per day. This repetition will make sure that the new word becomes firmly lodged in your memory. Using it in different contexts will keep your mind alert for opportunities, and will help increase your speed of thinking *and* your Creative Intelligence.

The simple mathematics of this procedure are also exciting: if your vocabulary is around the average of 1,000 words, in only one year you will have increased the power of your vocabulary by nearly 40 per cent (1,000 + 365 = **1,365**)!

If you continue this practice for 20 years, you will be eight times above the average (1,000 + (20 x 365 = 7,300) = **8,300**)!

Put your new words into an index file, and keep the "current five" on Post-It™ notes so that you can see them and review them on a daily basis before they enter your long-term memory.

If you are really intent and focused upon improving your Verbal Intelligence, you can up the number of new words per day. If you increase the number from one to five, then in two years you will have a vocabulary equivalent to the average top university graduate!

Even the sky is not the limit here, for your brain is capable of storing *billions* of words per year.

DID YOU KNOW?

The size of your vocabulary is highly related to your general success in life.

2. Play Verbal Games

In your leisure time play verbal games like Scrabble®, or do crossword puzzles or other similar word games and puzzles that are found in many daily newspapers and magazines. Play around with words with friends, make up poetry and stories – use your Creative Intelligence to its full!

3. Read Voraciously and Widely

Select for yourself your own reading course. Choose books on different subjects – history, drama, fiction, travel, exploration, whatever! Try to ensure that a

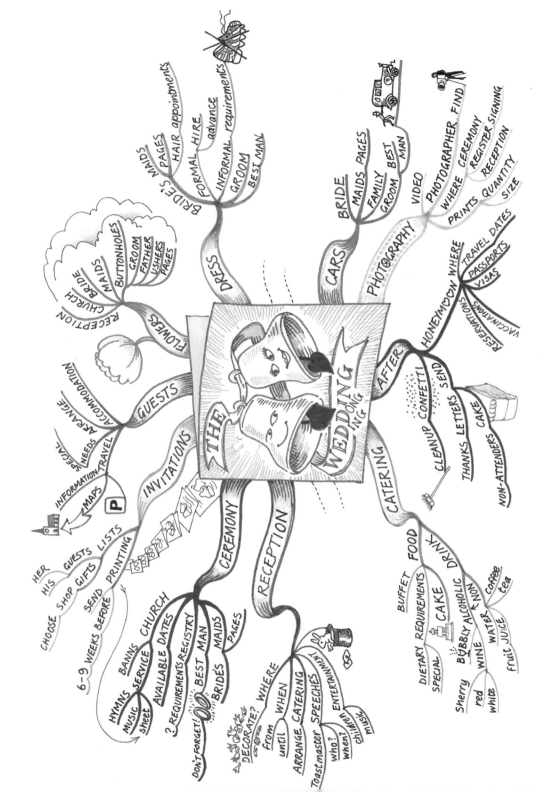

Plate 11

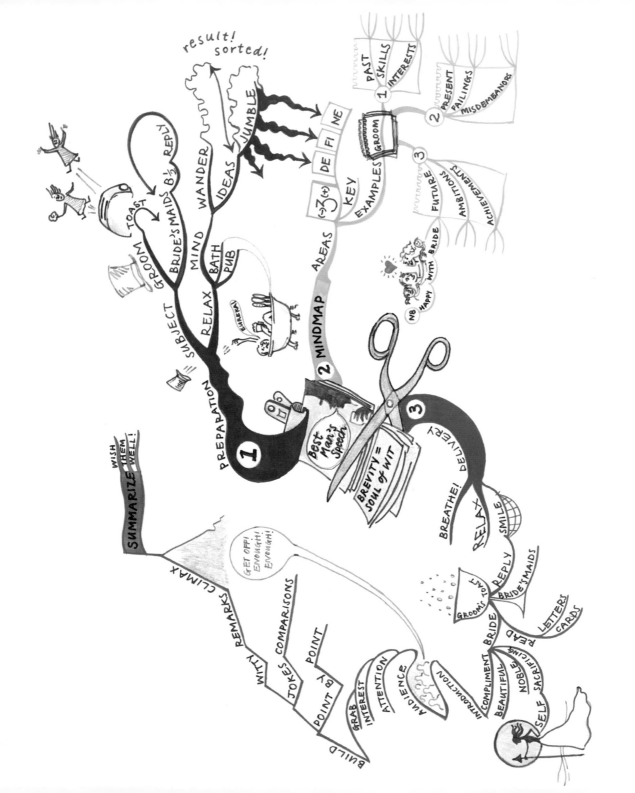

Plate 12

number of books stretch your brain – it will enjoy the exercise!

4. Buy a Pocket Dictionary

Keep it with you at all times so that you can look up any new, unfamiliar words that you come across during the day. A bigger dictionary at home to give in-depth background and explanations for all your new words is useful too.

5. Buy a Thesaurus

A thesaurus is a remarkable sort of book that lists all the words that have the same or similar meaning for any word you choose. Used in conjunction with your dictionary, a thesaurus is a wonderful way for "surfing" to find new and intriguing words that relate to ones you already know, and is great for expanding your vocabulary.

6. Learn to Speed Read

If you simply doubled your reading speed this week, you could, while still spending the same amount of *time* reading as you do now, read *twice* as many books as you would have done! An increased reading speed will also boost your verbal IQ.

Simple techniques for improving your speed include the following:

- Motivate yourself to read faster and you will.
- Look out for key words and ideas.
- Take in chunks of meaning rather than individual words.
- Keep the book a reasonable distance from your eyes.
- Guide your eyes by using something as a pointer (a pencil, pen, chopstick, etc.), which you move smoothly underneath the line you are reading.

7. Improve your Concentration

One of the most common situations in which people lose concentration is when they are reading. The main reason for this, apart from reading too slowly, is that they are not taking breaks regularly enough. When you are reading "hard" material such as instruction manuals, legal documents and other such "text," give your eyes and yourself regular breaks. Try underlining or highlighting key words with a marker pen as well, and your concentration will immediately improve.

Your Recall vs. Your Understanding

Most people, if they have been studying for 40 minutes and are having difficulty getting into the material, would, if they found themselves suddenly understanding it well, carry on until understanding decreased, and then take a break. Very few of us would take the risk of nipping our understanding "in the bud" by stopping.

Surprisingly, however, taking a break at this point would actually be the best thing to do. The reason for this is that the brain can continue to understand long after its ability to recall or bring back that information has started to decline. If you check your own experience, you will become aware of many instances in which you understood the information perfectly, only to forget it shortly thereafter.

Taking a break, which would seem to be a good way to lose concentration, actually *improves* it! The break gives your brain and body a chance to reorganize, reintegrate and recuperate, thereby improving the efficiency of your work, which in turn raises your motivational level, helps you solve problems more easily, reduces stress and increases your overall energy.

If your goal is to recall something that you are studying or are in some other way involved in remembering, you must make sure that your time is maximized. This time use coincides with the rest/activity cycle, in that a period of between 20 and 60 minutes of taking in information maximizes both understanding and recall. After 60 minutes, your understanding may continue, but recall will inevitably decline. Remember, taking a break allows your brain to integrate the material already learned, and to take a mental breather before going on to the next chunk.

When planning your intelligence-management and development system, it should become increasingly apparent that regular daily, weekly, monthly and yearly breaks are an *essential* part of any effective system. And the more you protest that you haven't got time for such things, the more you need them!

Your Break Menu

So what kind of breaks does your brain need? Basically anything that is different from the task it has been doing.

People have found the following to be useful and enjoyable. Take your pick!

- listening to music
- resting
- meditating
- exercising/stretching
- doing some short household task, like taking the dishes out of the machine
- dancing
- taking a short stroll
- doodling/drawing
- singing
- playing a musical instrument
- day-dreaming
- "just doing nothing"
- wandering round the yard.

Make sure that your break is a *real* break from the activity that you have been doing, and that it lasts for approximately 5 to 10 minutes.

8. Reading Words and Remembering Them

The reason why most people forget what they read is generally because they think they have to remember sentences. Your brain does *not* remember sentences!

Think about it. How many sentences can you remember that you have either read, spoken or heard in the last two weeks, which are of eight words or more in length? If you can remember more than 10 you are doing brilliantly and far better than average.

What your brain *remembers* are the key words. Having remembered these, your Creative and Verbal Intelligences come into play, and you literally recreate the information, scene or event you are describing to yourself or others.

Therefore, when you are reading and want to remember something, note down the important key words, arrange them into a Mind Map® with colors and images, and your memory of what you have read will improve immensely. If you review these notes after a week, then after a month, and then after a few months, you will find that your memory of the information will be virtually perfect! (This technique is especially good for remembering novels and their plots.)

9. Develop your Logical Thinking Powers

Logical thinking is, quite simply, understanding words, their meanings and, more especially, the relationship between them. It is this ability to understand the relationships between words that constitutes another part of your verbal IQ. Like vocabulary it can be learned and improved, and your skills in it sharpened.

The first way to develop this part of your Verbal Intelligence is to make a game of finding relationships between words (just like those that commonly appear in standard IQ tests), such as "dog is to cat as puppy is to ..." Many of the increasingly popular puzzle magazines regularly pose such brain teasers.

A second method of developing your logical Verbal Intelligence is to be on the lookout for errors in logical arguments, especially in newspapers and magazines, radio and television programmes, and in statements from scientific, business and political leaders.

A logical argument is one in which, *if the basic facts are true*, the conclusions that follow must also be true. Here are two logical thinking processes:

1   All As are B
    All Bs are C
    Therefore all As are C

2   All Bs are C
    A is a C
    Therefore A is a B

Do you think that they are:

    both correct?
    both incorrect?
    the first wrong, the second correct?
    the first correct, the second wrong?

If you said that number 1 was correct and number 2 was incorrect, you were right. Let's look first at the first argument. We need to start with a correct premise or assumption: all tarantulas (A) are spiders (B). You can follow this by all spiders (B) are eight-legged (C). The correct, logical conclusion therefore follows: all tarantulas (A) are eight-legged (C). This form of argument is only true if the original premise is correct.

If the premise is *incorrect* then this form of argument can mislead you dangerously, as the second example demonstrates: all berries (B) are good to eat (C); the Deadly Nightshade (A) is a berry (B); therefore the Deadly Nightshade (A) is good to eat (C)!

As you develop your Verbal Intelligence, be on the lookout for logical errors such as:

- where emotional language is used instead of facts
- where an authoritative figure is used to "prove" an argument when the authoritative figure might well be wrong
- where sources of information are defined in flowery terms but are not identified
- where apparent agreement is utterly contradicted by the use of the word "but"
- where definitions are subtly changed as an argument progresses.

Become like Sherlock Holmes in your use of vocabulary and logical thinking skills!

10. Developing your Word Power

Here is a "get started" exercise to help you develop your word power.

Powerful Verbs

Although we think we speak English, and that English is largely based on "Old English" or Anglo-Saxon, the fact is that very few words currently used in the English language can be traced back to Old England. More than 60 per cent of the words you have spoken this week, and have read in *Head First,* come from either Latin and Greek, or from the romance languages such as French and Italian.

In this word power-building exercise we are going to focus more on the Old English words, which tend to pack a more powerful verbal punch than the Latin and Greek words. For example, the Old English *walk* would be *perambulate* in Latin.

There follows some good, strong Old English words. Next to each are four choices of meaning. Choose the one you feel is nearest in meaning to the key word, then check your answers on page **213**.

1 **Cloy**

to fight

to tie up

to get sick of

to lie

2 **Flail**

to drown

to peel

to beat or floq

to mess something

3 **Flaunt**

to show off in a gaudy or vulgar manner

to hit someone with your fist

to dance energetically

to drink fast

4 **Flay**

to fail

to criticize strongly or to skin

to sail a boat fast

to speak a foreign language poorly

5 **Flout**

to be arrogant

to argue with someone

to shout

to treat with scorn and contempt

6 **Foist**

to jump off

to fly up

to "palm off" something almost criminally

to pull a rope

7 **Prate**

to rant or babble on foolishly

to parade up and down

to make out of metal

to sing like a bird

8 **Rail**

to construct a train

to complain loudly

to draw the line

to plant trees

9 **Raze**

to construct

to destroy, to demolish utterly, to level to the ground

to set fire to

to launch

10 **Wreak** (pronounced "reek")

to inflict a vengeance upon

to hit with a hammer

to make out of wood

to inflict as vengeance

11. Learn a New Language

Now that you know that every language contains roughly only a thousand words which are commonly used by most people in their daily writing and speaking, learning a new language should not appear nearly so daunting. To keep your language and verbal skills in tip-top condition, try learning a new language every 10 years or so. Learn the vocabulary first, then make the associations between the words. This is the way that babies – the best language learners in the world – do it! Grammar comes later.

By setting yourself this goal you will be opening up the horizons of your brain for its entire life. You will be keeping it constantly on the alert for new vocabulary and language learning opportunities. It is also a wonderful idea to supplement your language learning with visits to that country, and with books about its history and culture. These will help you develop your Social Intelligence and communication skills, your Sensory Intelligence and your Creative Intelligence (not to mention having fun and stimulating holidays!), at the same time as your Verbal Intelligence.

12. Make Words your Hobby

Wherever you can and it is appropriate, ask people for the meaning of unusual and unfamiliar words they might use. If possible, find out the derivations of the words as well. Make sure you keep a notebook handy, in which you can jot down new words that you hear in conversations, that appear in the media, or that you encounter in your general reading. These can be used as part of your Vocabulary Dietary Supplement! At the end of each week do a quick new-word review.

13. Learn the Different Parts of Words

Words often have prefixes (short additions such as "re-," or "per-" attached to the beginning of the word), or suffixes (little bits like "-able" tagged on the end). Knowing just one prefix can immediately multiply your vocabulary several times over.

For example, if you did not know that "uni" came from the Latin word meaning "one," then words such as "unicellular," "united," "uniform," "unit" and "unique" would all be difficult to understand. Once you do know the meaning of the prefix, everything becomes much clearer.

Similarly if you did not know that the suffix "able/ible" again came from the Latin and meant "capable of" or "fit for," then words like "durable," "enjoyable," "flexible" and "divisible" could be a bit obscure. When such prefixes and suffixes are known, the root words become clear, as will many other new words which you may have never known before. Because of your new awareness of the jigsaw pieces that go to make them up, words will suddenly become "comprehensible!"

Your Verbal Intelligence Questionnaire follows. Remember that a score of 50 per cent or more means that you are doing really well. A score of 100 per cent means that you are a genius in this intelligence. Check yourself over time to watch your scores rise, and enter them on the table on page **221**.

MULTIPLE INTELLIGENCE TEST – VERBAL INTELLIGENCE

For each of the following questions rank yourself on a scale of 0–100. A score of 0 would mean that the statement in no way whatsoever applies to you, and a score of 100 means that it describes you perfectly.

I have an extensive and far-ranging vocabulary that would be ranked in the top 1 per cent in the country (10,000+ words).   SCORE ......

I love words and everything to do with them.   SCORE ......

I enjoy reading and regularly read a wide range of books, magazines and other material.   SCORE ......

People tend to comment on my ability to express myself clearly and precisely with words. They will often combine this with comments about my high intelligence.   SCORE ......

I like to study both literature and language.   SCORE ......

Learning new languages is a skill about which I feel exceptionally confident.   SCORE ......

I enjoy theatre, including both witty and humorous plays.   SCORE ......

I both enjoy logic and logical expression, and am considered to be especially rational by my friends and colleagues.   SCORE ......

I take particular delight in such games and puzzles as Scrabble®
and crosswords.   ·   SCORE ......

I enjoy communicating and pride myself in my power to so do.   SCORE ......

                                                    TOTAL SCORE ......

As a little extra, here is a short Verbal Intelligence Skills test for you to do. (The answers are on page **214**.) Once again, repeat this test over a period of time, and watch your scores rise as your Verbal Intelligence increases.

Give yourself 15 minutes maximum to complete the 10 questions of your Verbal Intelligence Skills Test

VERBAL INTELLIGENCE SKILLS TEST

1 QUAD is to OCT as TRI is to...   (50 points)

2 Arrange the following letters to make four words: (100 points)
   RABIN
   HINTK
   ERATCEIV
   RETOCX

3 Fill in the missing word: (100 points)
   INFANT is to INFANCY
   as ADULT is to ....

4 Which is the odd word out?   (150 points)
   NOLI
   TERIG
   GROMNLE
   NELFEI
   ACT

5 Insert the missing letter: (100 points)

c

E   o

t

s

y

L

6 Insert the missing letter: a, d, h, m, s, ...

7 Sixteen : One   (50 points)
   as Pound : ...

8 Violin : Cello   (100 points)
   as Cello : ...

9 Island : Land   (100 points)
   as ... : water

10 Insert a word that means the same as the two words   (150 points)
   outside the brackets:
   STICK (...) WAGER

TOTAL SCORE ......

ANSWERS - Developing your Word Power

1 To get sick of

2 To beat or flog

3 To show off in a gaudy or vulgar manner

4 To criticize strongly or to skin

5 To treat with scorn and contempt

6 To "palm off" something

7 To rant or babble on foolishly

8 To complain loudly

9 To destroy, demolish or to level to the ground

10 To inflict as vengeance

That was difficult! Now that you know the correct meanings of these words, get yourself more familiar with them and their use by looking at the following sentences in which they occur.

- "I don't want to **cloy** my taste with too much dessert," said the already stuffed diner.
- She put on her entire collection of diamonds, and **flaunted** them at the charity ball.
- The rider said he was going to **flail** his poor horse for not winning the race.
- In Parliament the Leader of the Opposition attempted to **flay** the Prime Minister; he criticized him mercilessly.
- The young rebels decided to **flout** the laws of the country.
- The crook tried to **foist** a false "masterpiece" onto the amateur art dealer.
- She began to **prate** about his "great accomplishments" in a manner that made him look like a total idiot!
- The people who felt that they had been wronged began to **rail** against the authorities.
- Genghis Khan decided to **raze** the city he had just conquered.

- He then decided to **wreak** havoc on the neighbouring town.

Now that you have added these ten new words into your vocabulary, repeat them to yourself, saying them out loud and writing them down. By doing this you will be strengthening your memory by using your multiple intelligent senses of sight and sound. Try to use each word a minimum of five times in the coming week. If you do this they will become part of your long-term vocabulary.

ANSWERS – Verbal Intelligence Skills Test

1 SEX (quad = 4; oct = 8; tri = three; sex = 6)

2 BRAIN
   THINK
   CREATIVE
   CORTEX

3 Adulthood or maturity (*not* adultery!)

4 LION
   TIGER
   MONGREL
   FELINE
   CAT
   = MONGREL (all the others are related to the cat family)

5 G (the letters spell the word COGITATE)

6 Z (d is the third letter from a; h is the fourth from d, etc.)

7 OUNCE

8 BASS

9 LAKE

10 STAKE (the word "stake" can mean either a form of stick or a gambling bet)

ranking your

multiple intelligences

Remember the exercise in the Numerical Intelligence chapter on ranking your life's priorities? Below is the same exercise, but this time try ranking your multiple intelligences.

In the space below, rank the 10 multiple intelligences introduced in *Head First* in order of their current importance to you in your life. Give the number one ranking to the intelligence you consider the *most* important, and the number ten ranking to the intelligence you consider is currently your *least* important.

Ranking Reality

1

2

3

4

5

6

7

8

9

10

Ranking Ideal

Now that you have ranked reality, it is time to rank your ideal. Imagine that you are in *total* control of your life, and that you can do anything your heart so desires. Imagine what your ideal life would be like and what kind of things you would be doing every day and throughout the year. Run a little mental film of that ideal life, analyzing which of your 10 intelligences you are using as the days go by.

In the space below rank your 10 intelligences again, this time based on the ideal life you have just imagined. Give the number one ranking to the intelligence that you would *most* use in your ideal life; the number ten ranking to the intelligence you would *least* use in your ideal life.

1

2

3

4

5

6

7

8

9

10

Now that you have used your Numerical Intelligence to rank your *real* and *ideal* uses of your multiple intelligences, it is time to look at the percentages of time you *actually* spend using them, and the percentages of time you would *ideally* like to spend on them.

Run through in your mind the percentage of time you devote to each of your multiple intelligences in an average day and rank them below, with the intelligence you spend most of your time using ranked 1, and the one you use least ranked 10. Beside these figures, put down the time ranking of your use of your intelligences, this time based on your *ideal* life.

Intelligence	Real amount of time	% of time	Ideal amount of time	% of time

The purpose of this exercise is to examine the difference between your real and your ideal life. This will allow you to change the usage pattern of your intelligences so that the real more closely approximates (although it may never actually reach) the ideal.

Those who have done this exercise find that the areas in their lives where they are currently experiencing the most difficulties include:

- the areas they have ranked lowest
- the areas where there are the greatest discrepancies between the ideal and the real
- the areas where they experienced confusion sorting out percentage estimations.

The reason why it is useful for you to have this information is that your brain is a self-correcting mechanism and works much like a guided missile: as long as it has its target, and as long as it "knows" where it is going, when it senses that it is going off course it will automatically realign its path, constantly zeroing in more accurately on the desired target. If you therefore find yourself with major discrepancies between reality and your ideal world, don't be discouraged. Your brain will automatically register these on the subconscious level, and will start its own self-correcting programme, aided by your conscious self-management.

MULTIPLE INTELLIGENCE TESTS - SCORES TABLE

Date:					
Intelligence:	Scores	Scores	Scores	Scores	Scores
1 Creative					
2 Personal					
3 Social					
4 Spiritual					
5 Physical					
6 Sensual					
7 Sexual					
8 Numeric					
9 Spatial					
10 Verbal					
Totals					

future word

You are now about to launch your massive collection of intelligences onto the world and the future!

You might find it amusing, rewarding, productive and encouraging to revisit the questionnaires you completed as you progressed through *Head First*. If you have put any of the Brain Workout recommendations into practice, you should see some significant changes in your scores already.

Head First has been all about changing the modern trend from "Dumbing Down" to "Smartening Up." Now that you have reached the end of *Head First*, you should realize that you are as smart as you always suspected you were – and that's amazingly smart!

Similarly, every other person is amazingly smart too. The extraordinary work and skill of your fellow humans – constantly expressing their different intelligences – is something wonderful to marvel at. Classifying people simply as either "smart" or "dumb" does a gross injustice to you and to the person so labelled.

Remember – you are smarter than you think!

There is a nice story about the composer Beethoven and his brother.

The two of them used to write to each other regularly – Beethoven from wherever he was working at the time, his brother from his country estate.

His brother used to sign his letters with his name and then the description, "Landowner"; in reply Beethoven used to sign his letters, "Brain-owner."

Welcome to the brain-owners' club!

ABOUT THE AUTHOR

Tony Buzan is one of the world's leading thinkers, communicators and media Brain Stars. From very average academic beginnings, he worked on developing his own traditional IQ level, raising it to that of genius. He is the originator and creator of what has been described as the ultimate creative thinking tool – the Radiant Thinking Mind Map®, and is renowned world-wide for his talks on memory, creativity, learning, self-improvement and the brain, lecturing to audiences of all nationalities, ages and educational levels.

Tony Buzan has written and co-authored more than 80 books on the brain and learning, and is a member of Mensa, the high IQ society. He edited Mensa's International Journal – *Intelligence* – for three years, and has founded a number of organizations, such as The Brain Trust, and has started the World Championships of the Brain.

Tony Buzan is a known and respected poet, and takes part in competitive rowing and swimming matches. He is also a member of the Great Britain Olympic rowing coaching team.

BUZAN CENTRES

Learning & Thinking for the 21st Century

MAKE THE MOST OF YOUR MIND

- In-company Training
- Licensing for Companies and Independent Trainers
- "Open" Business and Public Seminars
- Educational Seminars

We are the ONLY organization that can license use of the Mind Maps® and associated trademarks

FOR FULL DETAILS OF BUZAN LEARNING SEMINARS

and information on our range of BrainFriendly® products, including:

- books
- software
- audio and video tapes
- support materials

SEND FOR OUR BROCHURE

CONTACT US AT:

Email: Buzan@Mind-Map.com
Website: www.Mind-Map.com

Or: Buzan Centres Inc. (Americas)
            PO Box 4, Palm Beach
            Florida
            FL 33480, USA

            Telephone: +1 561 881 0188
            Fax: +1 561 434 1682

            Buzan Centres Ltd (Rest of World)
            54 Parkstone Road
            Poole, Dorset BH15 2PG

            Telephone: +44 (0) 1202 674676
            Fax: +44 (0) 1202 674776

MAKE THE MOST OF YOUR MIND ... TODAY!

NOTES

NOTES

NOTES